Making Christian Choices in the Marketplace

Gregory Mellema

THE BOTTOM LINE

CRC Publications
Grand Rapids, Michigan

Acknowledgments

We are grateful to Gregory Mellema, professor of philosophy at Calvin College in Grand Rapids, Michigan, for writing this book. He has taught courses and seminars on business both at the college and in churches in the Grand Rapids area. In addition to a degree in Philosophy, he has an M.B.A. from the University of Michigan.

The Bottom Line
Making Christian Choices in the Marketplace

Library of Congress Cataloging-in-Publication Data

Mellema, Gregory, 1948-
[Business]
The bottom line: making Christian choices in the marketplace / Gregory Mellema.
p. cm. — (Issues in Christian living)
Previously published as: Business: Making Christian Choices. 1990.
Includes bibliographical references.
ISBN 1-56212-064-6: $6.50
1. Business ethics. 2. Christian ethics. 3. Business—Religious aspects—Christianity. I. Title. II. Series.
HF5387.M44 1994
174'.4—dc20 94-22303
CIP

10 9 8 7 6 5 4 3 2

CONTENTS

INTRODUCTION

"Can there be such a thing as business ethics?"

It's surprising how often people ask this question. Many of them ask it in jest, or half in jest, but others are quite serious. Some of them wonder whether ethics has any genuine relevance or applicability in the realm of business. Others—those who view business as an inherently evil or immoral human institution—are convinced that it does not.

This booklet assumes not only that there is such a thing as business ethics, but also that it's possible to approach such ethics in a distinctively Christian way. Business is one of many areas in life in which Christians are called to restore and transform culture in Christ's name, and thinking about a Christian approach to business ethics is an important first step in understanding how we can carry out this creation mandate.

Many people have already taken this first step. Virtually all readers of this book will be able to think of one or more leaders in the business community whose faith in God is the driving force in all of their business-related decisions—people who never allow their Christian convictions to be compromised in any way by what goes on in their business lives.

Aspiring to be like such people is part of what is involved in a study of business ethics. However, this booklet is not designed just for Christians in business-related careers. The issues it discusses are designed to be of interest to all Christians who are concerned about justice and fairness in the marketplace. Those in business-related careers will find guidance in discussing these issues. But these issues affect the lives of all Christians, and it is important for all of us to do some thinking about them.

This booklet does not attempt to present an exhaustive account of the issues in business ethics. Nor does it offer a set of ready-made solutions to the dilemmas that arise in discussions of business ethics. Rather, it provides an organized context for discussing these questions and suggests some frameworks for thinking about them.

The central focus of the discussion will be issues in Christian living. Within each lesson an attempt will be made to single out some important issues that Christians face as they deal with or are part of business organizations. The emphasis throughout will be upon issues that concern and affect Christians and that are profitable for Christians to discuss together.

Session 1 introduces the concept of business ethics and lays out a five-step procedure for dealing with ethical dilemmas. The issues treated in the remaining chapters are organized according to the responsibilities of the firm to its employees (session 2), the responsibilities of the employees to the firm (session 3), the responsibilities of the firm to consumers (session 4), and the responsibilities of the firm to other groups, such as shareholders, competitors, labor unions, governmental agencies, and the general public (session 5). The final lesson will examine Christian values in business and discuss some important ways in which a variety of firms are making an effort to promote a better sense of values in their organizations.

SESSION ONE

LOVING YOUR NEIGHBOR IN THE MARKETPLACE

A merchant is carrying grain to a town that is suffering a severe famine. He knows that the starving townspeople will be eager to pay a high price for his grain. However, he also knows that other merchants are on their way with more grain. Does he have a moral obligation to inform the townspeople that more grain is on the way? Or is it his right to remain silent and thereby command a higher price?

On the one hand, the merchant may believe that the townspeople have a right to know that more grain is on the way; he may feel that he has no right to exploit their misfortune. On the other hand, he might reason that their ignorance is not his concern; his job is to sell his grain at the highest price the market will bear.

For many centuries people have been confronting moral dilemmas in business. This story of the grain merchant is recounted by the Roman statesman Cicero in the first century B.C., and he does not hesitate to offer his solution to the dilemma. According to Cicero, the ethical thing to do is to inform the people that more grain is on the way. The merchant, says Cicero, has a moral *duty* to convey this information to the townspeople.

As with many moral dilemmas, however, in this one there is room for honest disagreement. In one of the earliest business-ethics disputes on record, Thomas Aquinas comments on Cicero's discussion of the grain merchant and refuses to accept the conclusion that the merchant is obligated to reveal that grain will soon be plentiful. It would be morally commendable or praiseworthy for the merchant to inform the people that more grain is on the way, Aquinas believes, but the merchant is not morally obliged to do so. Informing the people would be going beyond the call of duty.

In the grain-merchant dilemma, the seller possesses valuable information that the buyer is unaware of. Often, however, the reverse is true, as in a dilemma faced by the Metropolitan Museum of New York in October, 1965.

A private New York art gallery acquired a 26-inch stucco sculpture that its appraisers said was of little value. While the bust was on display, experts from the Metropolitan Museum of Art quietly carried on an investigation of the sculpture and concluded that the gallery's appraisers were wrong: the sculpture was an original work of either Andrea de Verocchio or Leonardo de Vinci.

Subsequently, at one of the gallery's routine auctions, gallery officials started the bidding on the sculpture at $150, a clear signal to the museum's buyer that gallery owners had accepted their appraisers' original judgment and were unaware of the bust's actual worth. Perhaps Cicero would argue that like the grain merchant, the museum experts had a moral obligation to inform the gallery of their beliefs concerning the bust. Others might argue, following Thomas Aquinas, that sharing such information would be a nice, praiseworthy thing to do, but one who did so would be exceeding the call of duty. Indeed, some might go on to say that it would be downright foolish for the museum to share this information; business is simply not conducted that way.

Evidently the museum shared this latter view, for its representatives proceeded to bid on the bust and were able to acquire it for $225. A short time later one expert estimated its actual worth at about $500,000.

A Place for Christian Conscience?

Sometimes it is difficult to know how to go about solving moral dilemmas such as these—especially for Christians. We look to Scripture for answers, but are uncertain how to apply God's Word to our particular situation.

Some might argue, for example, that what the Metropolitan Museum did was a form of bearing false witness: through their silence they deceived the gallery about the value of the bust. However, while it is true that in some cases silence can be equated with bearing false witness, I suspect that many Christians would think it unreasonable to condemn the museum on these grounds. Similarly, it is uncertain whether the silence of the grain merchant could be construed as a clear instance of bearing false witness. At least one thoughtful Christian, Thomas Aquinas, did not think so.

The discussion of issues in business ethics has not always been a high priority among Protestant Christians. But as relationships between business organizations and our modern society become increasingly complex, Christians must take a stand. We must begin to wrestle with some of the important ethical questions that business raises in our world.

Christians who are employed in large business organizations, for example, often find that their actions are so intertwined with the actions of their coworkers that it is difficult to evaluate who is responsible for either the good or the evil that come from their company. The dynamics of decision-making can become exceedingly complex. Anyone who tries to evaluate the moral status of his or her own individual role in these complex group interactions is faced with an overwhelming task.

Unfortunately, those who are employed in large corporations often face enormous pressure to subordinate their personal ethical standards to those of the organization. A survey of three thousand executives by the American Management Association found that most felt they were under pressure to compromise their own ethical standards to meet company goals. The modern business organization places great emphasis on results, often narrowly measured in terms of money. Thus, as firms become larger and more decentralized, performance tends to be measured in numbers, and the pressure to meet the goals of the firm can become intense.

In his book *The Executive Conscience*, Albert Carr relates a conversation with one successful executive in a large corporation. The man told Carr that someone in a job like his could not afford the luxury of a conscience in the office. He added with a sigh that he envied his associates whose consciences had never developed beyond the Neanderthal stage and who had no difficulty in accepting things as they were.

Carr states that people in general are becoming increasingly distrustful of business morality. In one survey, nearly half of the two thousand Americans polled said that they believe that most people in business will try anything, honest or dishonest, for a buck. In another study, a large majority of students in colleges and universities across the country indicated that they were convinced that business is a dog-eat-dog affair. Some of those surveyed regarded this as a reason to stay away from a business career. But many others actually viewed it as an incentive to enter the business world.

A survey of business executives revealed that, although 90 percent regarded themselves as ethical, fully 80 percent could point to numerous generally accepted practices in their industry which they personally regarded as unethical. These practices included bribery of government officials, price rigging, and collusion in contract bidding. Carr reports that in the U.S. the kickback is taken so much for granted that the Internal Revenue Service now provides detailed instructions for reporting the income from this source.

Clearly the time is right for people to think seriously about ethical issues in business. Christians employed in business organizations can no longer assign business ethics a low priority.

Three Approaches to Doing Business Ethically

The term *business ethics* can be defined as the systematic study of what is good or bad, right or wrong, praiseworthy or blameworthy, in one's business conduct. Sometimes a person's business conduct can be evaluated by appealing to ordinary codes of ethics, as when people condemn someone who attempts to gain a competitive advantage by telling blatant lies about a product. But ordinary codes of ethics often give little insight in evaluating the behavior that occurs within the context of complex business organizations. Thus, it is not altogether clear whether the Metropolitan Museum, in our previous example, can be accused of a form of lying. To deal with tricky questions such as these, a solid system of business ethics is essential.

What *is* the basis for deciding whether an act is good or bad, right or wrong, praiseworthy or blameworthy in one's business conduct? Modern ethics has traditionally provided us with two answers to this question.

But My Motives Were Good

One of the traditional approaches has grown out of the work of the German philosopher Immanuel Kant, who believed one should concentrate upon the *will* or *motives* of the moral agent. If someone acts out of a good will or on the basis of good motives, then (all other things being equal) the act itself can be regarded as basically good.

If my motives are good in selling you a power mower which, through your own failure to operate it properly, causes damage to your expensive shrubbery, then I cannot be faulted for selling it to you. On the other hand, if my intent is to harm you or your property as the result of your purchasing the mower, then selling you the mower is wrong.

According to this approach, the Metropolitan Museum acted ethically if its motives were good (making the bust available for its visitors to view) and unethically if its motives were bad (swindling the private gallery).

What is striking about the Kantian approach is its failure to say anything about the results or consequences of one's action. No matter how much damage or suffering result from an act performed out of good or pure motives, the act is still regarded as basically good. Conversely, an act performed out of bad motives can never be praised on moral grounds, no matter how much good it produces.

But It Did So Much Good

A second traditional approach, known as utilitarianism, emphasizes the importance of *consequences.* According to this approach, the right action is the one that benefits the greatest number of people. The basic idea is that instead of seeking to boost our own self-interests, we should be constantly concerned with the interests of society at large. Utilitarians, then, believe that the test of whether an act is right or wrong is the degree to which it benefits society.

What is striking about utilitarianism is its failure to say anything about good motives. To the utilitarian it is not important whether an act proceeds from good motives. As long as an act brings the greatest benefits to the greatest number, it is considered a right action.

Perhaps it was the art gallery's intent to pass off what it considered to be a worthless bust for whatever price it could get. Nevertheless, the sale of the bust brought great benefits to the Metropolitan Museum and the community at large. So on utilitarian grounds the gallery is to be praised for what it did—even though its motives were less than honorable.

Conversely, utilitarians condemn an act that, although performed out of the best of motives, ends up harming society. The U.S. Steel Company, for example, claims that it was acting out of the best of motives when it purchased Marathon Oil for $5.93 billion in 1983, Husky Oil for $488 million in 1984, and Texas Oil and Gas for $3.03 billion in 1985. The company claims that these acquisitions were necessary for its financial well-being.

However, critics charge that if U.S. Steel had used these funds to modernize its steel plants instead of purchasing oil companies, several of its plant closings in Ohio and Pennsylvania could have been avoided. Hence the company can be condemned on utilitarian grounds for taking a course of action that closed down plants and brought harm to thousands of employees who were laid off.

Putting the Two Together

Surely the Kantians are right to emphasize the importance of a good will, and utilitarians are right to call attention to the importance of benefiting society. However, the two views fail in that they do not recognize the importance of the other's argument.

In the Sermon on the Mount Jesus speaks about good trees bearing good fruit and bad trees bearing bad fruit (Matt. 7:17). It is one thing to be a good tree, and it is another thing to bear good fruit. Of course, good trees typically bear good fruit, but it is still possible to distinguish the goodness of the tree from the goodness of its fruit.

Jesus' words seem to indicate that two things are important in the moral evaluation of a person's actions. First, there is the state or disposition of the person who is acting. Sometimes people act from a good nature and sometimes from an evil nature. Here Kant's advice is relevant: it is important for one's will or motives to be good.

Second, it is important to ask whether one's actions succeed in bearing good fruit. As the utilitarian contends, it is important that one's actions benefit society.

The passage seems to indicate, then, that it is important for a Christian to be concerned about both motives *and* consequences. People can be criticized for their evil motives, even when the fruit of their works is good. And people who act out of good motives can still be criticized for harming others. It is not enough for a tree simply to be good, and it is not enough simply to bear good fruit. Both are of critical importance.

Garrett's Guidelines

But how exactly does one go about deciding how to act? In areas not specifically addressed by the Scriptures, how can a person determine whether a given course of action is ethical or unethical? Christians employed in business organizations frequently express uncertainty about whether they are doing the right thing. Where can they find helpful answers?

Obviously, there is no perfectly worked out set of guidelines to give clear answers to all the moral perplexities a person might encounter in the marketplace. However, it may be helpful to examine briefly a set of general guidelines offered by Christian author Thomas Garrett in his book *Business Ethics*. Garrett's guidelines, which embody the spirit of Christian morality, offer five tests a Christian may use to determine whether an act is morally permissible.

Before explaining his tests, Garrett makes a distinction between major and minor evils in the business world. He defines major evils as those that "strike at the very dignity of the human being" or "involve the destruction of goods necessary for an individual or society." Major evils, then, are such things as asking an employee or client to compromise his or her moral integrity, conducting unreasonable searches of an employee's person or personal property, or instituting mass layoffs in an area that is already economically distressed.

The tests that Garrett recommends incorporate this distinction between major and minor evils.

Test One

Perform no action in which any evil, major or minor, is willed as an end in itself.

It is obviously wrong to will evil for its own sake, no matter what the circumstances might be. Thus, it is unethical to dismiss an employee solely to bring harm to him or her or to reprimand an employee solely for the purpose of humiliation. Likewise, it is clearly wrong for a large firm to switch suppliers for no other reason than to exact revenge for some alleged wrongdoing by their present supplier. According to test one, it is never right to exact revenge.

Test Two

Perform no action in which any major evil is willed as a means to an end.

It is never permissible to will a major evil in order to attain a good end. Most cases of extortion and bribery are ruled out by this test. By offering a bribe, I am willing that another person compromise his or her moral integrity as a stepping-stone toward my own end.

Test Three

Perform no action in which any minor evil is willed as a means to an end, unless there is a proportionate reason for doing so.

The concept of proportionality is a bit complicated, but the basic idea involves weighing the evil features of an act over against the good features. Thus, one may will a minor evil, according to Garrett, if the good that is realized outweighs the evil.

In order to build a new plant, for example, one might will that certain trees be removed. And in order to run a successful operation, a store manager might will that his clerks fill out lengthy reports (which he knows they despise) whenever a customer returns merchandise. In these cases a manager wills a minor evil, but has proportionate reasons for doing so.

On the other hand, willing that certain pollutants be released in order to produce goods as economically as possible does not, in all probability, satisfy the proportionality requirement.

Test Four

Perform no action in which any of the risked side effects which are foreseen as possible are evil, unless there is a proportionate reason for doing so.

The first three tests are concerned primarily with one's will or motives. Test four, by contrast, deals with the unintended consequences of actions, and it is here that utilitarian considerations become relevant. According to test four, risk-taking is sometimes morally permissible. In the earlier example of my selling you a power mower, I am taking a risk that you might use the mower to cause a great deal of damage. But it would be unreasonable to conclude that, based on this reason, it is always unethical to sell people power mowers.

On the other hand, test four rules out certain courses of action that involve taking risks. Suppose a drug manufacturer knows that a certain drug will probably have harmful side effects. The manufacturer might argue that since stopping production of the drug would mean laying off several hundred people, it is ethical to market the drug. However, saving several hundred jobs is almost certainly not a proportionate reason for proceeding to market a dangerous drug.

Test Five

Perform no action that passes tests three or four if there is an equally good method of attaining the same desired end which necessitates lesser evil.

Ethical behavior demands an awareness of alternative courses of action. Where an alternative can eliminate or minimize evil, an agent is no longer permitted to perform the original action.

A Positive Summary

Although Garrett's five tests do not speak to every conceivable situation, they can often provide significant help to a person who is struggling to make moral decisions. If an action seems clearly to pass all five of the tests, one can be reasonably certain that it is not unethical.

However, the five tests are not enough. No doubt, we need such guidelines to help us decide what we should *not* do. But in responding to God's call, rigid obedience to a set of rules about what we should avoid is not enough. Living a life of moral purity should be a genuinely *positive* experience, filled with joy. As true disciples of Christ we should desire to follow the example he set for us while on earth.

It is noteworthy that Christ states his summary of the Ten Commandments in a positive fashion: we are to love God, and we are to love our neighbor. For a Christian in business, loving one's neighbor involves many things. It involves endeavoring to satisfy the genuine needs of society and treating everyone with the dignity that befits him or her as an imagebearer of God. And it involves the realization that we are part of a society of interdependent individuals, serving each other with the various gifts God has given us (1 Pet. 4:10).

SUGGESTIONS FOR GROUP SESSION

Opening

Be sure to read the introduction to this course to get an idea of the various aspects of business ethics that you will be discussing together during the weeks to come. Begin this first session together by taking time to introduce yourselves to one another, perhaps briefly describing the business or work situations you are (or have been) a part of. Each person may also want to say a few words about why he or she is interested in a discussion about business ethics.

Next read 1 Peter 4:10–11, a passage that talks about faithfully using the gifts God has given us in the service of others. Reflect briefly together on how we might use our gifts in business. Then open with prayer, mentioning some of the situations and concerns that have brought your group together to talk about ethics in business.

For Discussion

1. Discuss the choice the grain merchant faced. Cicero believed the merchant had a moral obligation to inform the townspeople that more grain was on the way; Thomas Aquinas believed he had no moral obligation to do so. Whose opinion seems more plausible and why? In evaluating this situation it may help to think of it in terms of a present-day scenario that involves supply and demand.
2. Would the grain merchant's decision not to inform the people pass Garrett's test five? What alternative course of action might he take that would require a lesser evil?
3. Defend or critique the Metropolitan Museum's method of obtaining the statue. As you prepare your argument, keep in mind the end result: the bust is now mounted in the museum for the public to enjoy free of charge. In what ways might a Christian assess this transaction differently than a non-Christian?

4. At a garage sale you see what you know to be a valuable antique worth several thousand dollars. It has a ten-dollar price tag on it. Is it ethical to purchase the antique for ten dollars, or are you morally obligated to inform the seller of the antique's value? Can or cannot a Christian in good conscience take advantage of the seller's ignorance in situations of this type? Why or Why not?
5. Put yourself back in the garage-sale dilemma. Would it make a difference whether the seller were poor or well-to-do? For example, the seller might be an elderly widow on a fixed income, but he might also be a financial wizard who made a fortune on Wall Street. In what ways is and/or is not the garage-sale dilemma the same as the dilemma the Metropolitan Museum faced at the auction?
6. In 1985 Lederle Labs was the sole manufacturer of whooping cough vaccine. Three other firms stopped producing the vaccine because of lawsuits and liability claims. Unfortunately, in 1985, 150 liability cases were also directed at Lederle Labs, charging that its vaccine caused brain damage. The company claimed that government, university, and corporate studies proved that there was no scientific basis for these charges. Nevertheless, in several cases juries awarded large damages to the claimants, and eventually Lederle Labs announced that it, too, would stop producing the drug.

   Although the incidence of whooping cough is now very low, the illness is always debilitating and sometimes life-threatening. Considering these facts and the lawsuits Lederle Labs faced, evaluate their decision using Garrett's five tests. Consider whether the threat of lawsuits constituted proportionate reason for discontinuing production of this important vaccine.
7. Radar detectors, or "fuzzbusters," enable drivers to know when they have entered a radar field. The drivers then have an opportunity to moderate the speed of their vehicles before their speed can be calculated by the police. In most states and provinces using a radar detector is illegal. However, in these same areas, manufacturing and selling fuzzbusters is perfectly legal.

   Use Garrett's five tests to determine whether it is ethical for Christians to manufacture, sell, or use radar detectors.

Closing

Conclude your session with a short prayer, asking God to make your motives pure and to lead you into actions that benefit others and avoid harmful consequences.

RESOURCES FOR FURTHER STUDY

Forell, George and William Lazareth. *Corporation Ethics*. Philadelphia: Fortress Press, 1980.

Garrett, Thomas and Thomas Klonoski. *Business Ethics*. Englewood Cliffs, NJ: Prentice-Hall, 1986.

Hosmer, LaRue Tone. *The Ethics of Management.* Homewood, Illinois: Irwin Publishing, 1987.

Roels, Shirley J. *Christians and Economic Life.* Grand Rapids, MI: Calvin College (Occasional Papers Series, Vol. 8, No. 1), 1990.

SESSION TWO

HONOR YOUR EMPLOYEE

In August, 1984 *Business Week* magazine reported that in a landmark court decision, three supervisory employees of Film Recovery Systems were judged responsible for the death of Stephan Golab, a fifty-nine-year-old fellow employee. Golab, a Polish immigrant who knew little English, died from cyanide poisoning after working for two months over open pits of fuming cyanide.

Those found responsible for Golab's death were Steven O'Neill, president of the company, Charles Kirschbaum, the plant supervisor, and Daniel Rodriguez, the plant foreman. The prosecution charged the three with being fully aware of the life-threatening dangers of breathing cyanide fumes and doing nothing to improve the working conditions. In particular, they failed to warn or protect workers who, like Stephan Golab, could not read English.

Employee Rights

Today, more than in any other period in history, employees are aware that the firms that hire them are responsible for their safety and well being. Workers have rights, and these rights are increasingly spelled out by legislation, union contracts, and company policies.

The case of Stephan Golab is a blatant example of an employee's rights being violated. In such cases it is not at all difficult to arrive at a clear moral judgment. Employers who are aware that their employees are working in life-threatening circumstances and fail to protect them are scarcely in a position to argue that they have done nothing unethical.

But in many other instances it is more difficult to determine whether the behavior of the employer or the firm is unethical. When the employer breaks no laws or written agreements (and clearly not everything which is unethical is a violation of human law), it is more difficult to arrive at a clear moral verdict.

Consider Adolph Coors Brewery's 1977 decision to use lie-detector tests in the hiring of new employees. The decision was prompted by two incidents: the discovery of a bomb in a Coors plant in August, 1977, and the kidnapping and murder of a member of the Coors family several years earlier. Chairman William Coors and his brother, Joseph Coors, were determined not to hire any person who might again endanger their families or their employees, and they believed a polygraph test would reduce the likelihood of hiring such a person.

In a notarized affidavit, Coors employees claimed to have been asked the following questions under the scrutiny of the lie detector:

1. Do you get along with your wife?
2. What is your sex preference?
3. Are you a communist?
4. Do you have money in the bank?
5. Have you ever stolen anything?
6. Do you know of any reason that you could be blackmailed?

In response to this new procedure, the members of Brewery Workers Local No. 366 walked off their jobs at the Adolph Coors Brewery Plant in Golden, Colorado. They believed the employment process was demeaning and degrading to potential employees. Coors responded by drawing up a standard questionnaire consisting of the following seven questions in an attempt to upgrade the new procedure:

1. Did you tell the complete truth on the employment application?
2. Have you ever used any form of illegal drug or narcotic on the job?
3. Has the use of alcohol frequently impaired your ability to perform on the job?
4. Are you concealing any information about subversive, revolutionary, or communistic activity?
5. Are you applying for a job with this company so that you can do it or any of its employees harm?

6. Are you presently wanted by the authorities for a felony?
7. Have you ever stolen any kind of merchandise, material, or money from an employer?

If the applicant had any hesitations about answering these questions under the scrutiny of the lie detector, he or she was invited ahead of time to discuss them. The applicant was assured that these were the only questions he or she would be asked.

In response to this "compromise" by Coors, the employees eventually called off the wildcat strike. The standard questionnaire procedure continued until the company decided in August, 1986, to stop mandatory polygraph testing of new employees.

Was it unethical for Coors to require its new employees to answer either the original set of questions or the standardized set? Applying Garrett's five tests, one might first ask whether the hiring process constituted a major evil. It is likely that those staging the wildcat strike thought the original set of questions did. If the hiring process was so demeaning that it struck at the very dignity of the job applicant, Garrett's second test would rule it out as unethical, no matter how much good it brought about for the firm.

On the other hand, if the hiring process constituted only a minor evil, one must go on to ask whether the brewery had a proportionate reason for initiating it. Surely the Coors brothers thought the kidnapping and bomb-planting incidents were proportionate reason. But did those incidents indeed justify precautions such as these?

Proceed with Caution

In a case of this nature there is room for honest disagreement. However, it is important for Christians to be particularly sensitive about upholding and preserving the dignity of the individual. When there is any question about whether a policy violates an employee's dignity, a Christian employer is well advised to err on the side of caution.

Christians must keep in mind that human dignity is rooted in a person's status as an image-bearer of God. Employers can almost always find an excuse to invade the privacy of an employee, but they should never do so without sound reasons.

It seems doubtful that the Adolph Coors Brewery had proportionate reasons for the procedures that they initiated. However, even if their decision to introduce these procedures passes Garrett's test three, it is questionable whether it passes test five. Could the company have taken an alternative course of action that would have served the same purpose and yet been less demeaning to their prospective employees? Since 1986 the company has in fact put in place a new procedure which appears to be just such an alternative.

However, the Adolph Coors Brewery was not alone in requiring polygraph tests. A study by the United States Senate estimates that 200,000 to 300,000 lie-detector tests are administered each year by firms in the United States. Two other surveys indicate that the loyalty of about one worker in every five is checked by eavesdropping or other means. These reports led David Ewing, in his book *Freedom Inside the Organization* (New York: E.P. Dutton, Inc., 1977, 131), to comment:

> According to an old Chinese saying, the buyer needs a thousand eyes, the seller but one. Personnel officials apparently have another version of this thought. Some of them say: the employer needs a thousand eyes, the employee but one.

The Employer's Dilemma

For many Christian employers, the issues under consideration pose a dilemma. On the one hand, one cannot always take the honesty of one's employees for granted. And it is the employer's right to provide for some measure of security precautions. Indeed, one might say it is the right of the employee to be spared the temptation of unethical conduct through the presence of security precautions.

On the other hand, the more effective these security precautions are designed to be, the greater the likelihood that they will become a demeaning invasion of privacy. Many large stores, for example, use surveillance equipment to monitor the behavior of both customers and employees. But sometimes employers are tempted to carry this surveillance one step further. They install microphones in the employees' lounge or restroom areas, suspecting that incidents of employee wrongdoing might be the subject of conversation during breaks. It is clear that the use of such microphones poses a significant invasion of the employees' privacy. It is hard to imagine how an employer might make a case for such an invasion of privacy, no matter how much employee misconduct is occurring.

Some hospitals conduct occasional, unannounced searches of employees' lockers and purses. While it might be argued that this practice serves to prevent the theft of equipment, these searches, too, come dangerously close to striking at the dignity of the person.

All things considered, it seems preferable for Christian employers to err on the side of trust than to risk violating a person's dignity. Purse and locker checks are not generally illegal if carried out in a reasonable manner, but the legality of such searches should not be the only consideration for a Christian who wishes to treat his or her employees with dignity and respect.

An Honorable Way to Discharge?

The discharge of employees is another area in which employers must refrain from violating the employee's dignity. An article on page 1 of the *Wall Street Journal* of April 24, 1982, describes an internal investigation by General Motors of employees suspected of engaging in a scheme to defraud the firm. The employees were never told that they were under investigation; one day they were simply called to General Motors' Tarrytown, New York, offices:

> Only a few days remained until Christmas, and [they] . . . were looking forward to the long paid holiday—totally unprepared for the ordeal most of them were about to face. Suddenly, without warning, about 25 salaried employees were summoned one by one. They were each funneled through a three room 'assembly line' where solemn-faced GM officials from Detroit fired them, stripped them of their company cars and other benefits, and gave them cab fare home. One worker, with more than 20 years of service, recalls watching in disbelief as a GM functionary with a map and a ruler measured out the distance to his home and handed him $15.

The author of the article describes the scenario as "an almost ruthless brand of corporate justice."

While General Motors had reason to believe that these employees were engaged in a scheme to defraud the company, they also may have had an ethical obligation to be more sensitive to the matter of due process.

In recent years it has become common through corporate mergers and takeovers for drastic numbers of workers to lose their jobs. "This human cost is not always figured in when top executives, investment bankers, and take-over lawyers concoct big deals that are increasingly part of the normal course of business," *Fortune* magazine reported a few years ago (July 9, 1984, p. 44).

The takeover of Gardner-Denver is a typical case in point:

> Cooper Industries, an industrial machinery manufacturer, has a reputation for handling acquisitions roughly. After its 1979 takeover of Gardner-Denver . . . Cooper shut down the corporate headquarters, decentralized the company, reduced employment in lackluster operations, shrank benefits, and cut working capital. Plenty of human flotsam bobbed in the wake.

It is difficult to make any universal ethical pronouncements about whether it is right or wrong to terminate employees when a merger or takeover occurs. But frequently these firings are carried out in a cruel and inhumane manner. In his book *Ethics of Management*

(Homewood, Illinois: Irwin, 1987, 30–31), LaRue T. Hosmer cites the case of Portland Machine Company, an industrial conglomerate, terminating an employee of 33 years. In an interview with Professor Hosmer, a son of this employee described the events as follows:

> About a week after Portland bought the company, one of their hotshots walked into Dad's office and told him he was through; said his performance had been "unacceptable" . . . . I remember enough about freshman economics to know that compressors are an industrial product, and that industrial sales are cyclical. You wait until the bottom of the cycle, and everyone's performance looks bad.
>
> Dad got 11 weeks' severance pay; no pension because he left before he was 60, and no medical insurance. At age 58 Dad is out looking for work, and you know he's not going to find anything. Fortunately, my brother and I can help Mom and Dad, but this has just about destroyed him. He is a decent, hard-working man who devoted his life to a company, and some M.B.A. can come in and say, "Get out."
>
> The really incredible part is that Dad's secretary, who has been with him for over 20 years, began to cry as she watched him start to leave. So they fired her. She doesn't have any children to help her; instead she was supporting her mother. . . .
>
> Sure, you can build profits if you cut people: the ones who are left will work twice as hard to be able to stay. And if you cut the older people, you save lots of money on the pension obligations and medical insurance. But, what a way to do it. Is this what you teach at the business school?

Firms have frequently terminated large numbers of employees with no advance warning whatsoever. A celebrated instance is the mass termination of five thousand workers by the Lykes-Youngstown Sheet and Tube Company in Youngstown, Pennsylvania. With no advance notice of any kind, these workers were told their jobs no longer existed.

It's true that sometimes firms do find it necessary to terminate large numbers of employees, but there is a right and a wrong way to do so. Fortunately, the U.S. has now passed legislation that makes some type of advance warning mandatory. But again, the broader ethical issue is one of treating employees with dignity and respect. Christian employers, in particular, must never lose sight of the human dimension when it becomes necessary to lay-off or terminate workers.

Perhaps Christian employers can set a good example by bending over backward to guarantee that the workers they let go are dealt with in as humane a way as possible. For example, some firms have hired outplacement services for the employees they have terminated. At the very least good ethics seem to demand that two things take place: (1) Due process for employees who are the objects of suspicion, and (2) advance warning for those who are the victims of lay-offs and firings.

The law has surprisingly little to say about firing employees and for the most part permits an employer to dismiss workers virtually at will. In one bizarre case an employee was fired for reasons which were challenged in a court of law. The judge ordered the company to reorder the employee, but he was immediately refired, and the second time the court upheld the dismissal. It therefore seems clear that the legality or illegality of a case of dismissal is not a good indicator of whether it is ethical or unethical.

Deciding Who to Hire

Great ethical abuses have also occurred in the areas of hiring and promoting. However, here the law has a good deal more to say, and many of the worst abuses of the past have ceased to occur. Because of civil rights legislation, for example, there is far less discrimination against prospective employees on the basis of their race than there was a generation ago.

However, many groups of people are not currently protected by anti-discrimination laws. In his book on business ethics, Manuel Valasquez gives several examples:

1. Liberty Mutual Insurance refused to hire a certain male simply because he was "effeminate," and a court upheld its actions.
2. Budget Marketing, Inc., fired a male who began to dress as a female prior to a sex-change operation, and a court upheld its action.
3. Many firms refuse to hire those who have acquired immune deficiency syndrome (AIDS). Some companies have fired or cancelled the health benefits of their employees who were discovered to have AIDS.
4. Philadelphia Electric Company refused to hire a woman for no other reason than that she weighed three hundred pounds. Many firms have policies against hiring overweight persons, and in most states this is perfectly legal.

The point is not that each of these examples is a case of clear moral wrongdoing. One might well argue, for example, that Budget

Marketing was perfectly justified in firing the man who began dressing as a woman. The point is that unjust discrimination can occur in a variety of forms, and sometimes it is easy to practice such discrimination without realizing it.

Employers of even very small businesses are faced with these and other similar dilemmas when hiring. Is it unethical to refuse to hire an applicant for no other reason than that he or she is overweight? Is it unethical to refuse to hire an applicant for no other reason than that he or she is not heterosexual, or was once indicted (but not convicted) for a crime? And, perhaps closer to home, is it unethical to refuse to hire an applicant for no other reason than that he or she is not a member of the same church denomination as all of one's other employees? No doubt many readers of this discussion guide have faced questions of this nature.

Naturally, the answers to all of these questions depend upon one's particular circumstances. It is obvious that a modeling agency, for example, might have good reasons for concern over the weight of its models, and there are no doubt situations in which it would be highly inappropriate to hire a gay person. But, once again, one's hiring policies and interviewing demeanor should never be degrading or demeaning to the applicant.

"Human Beings Came Instead"

Employers are also responsible for maintaining a good moral climate for their employees. As most employers discover, this is not as easy as it sounds. Establishing and maintaining a positive moral climate requires thoughtful deliberation in the development of a policy statement and a careful plan.

The employer also exerts a great deal of influence and control over the degree to which employees can find a sense of fulfillment and self-worth in their work. A proper concept of work and work atmosphere requires an awareness and understanding of human beings and their needs. Because of the amount of time and energy they spend on the job, people tend to identify themselves with the work they do. If their work does not give them an overall feeling of self-worth, their self-image is significantly diminished.

Frequently, employers and supervisors seem to have little or no understanding of the importance of morale. As the Swiss novelist and playwright Max Frisch once wrote, "We sought workers, and human beings came instead." Many employers would just as soon forget that their workers are human beings with human needs.

In his encyclical *Mater et Magistra*, the late Pope John XXIII commented on the need for workers to feel that they are an important part of the overall operation:

> Like our predecessors, we are convinced of the legitimacy of the workers' ambitions to take part in the life of the understanding in which they are employed . . . workers must be given an active part to play in the concern in which they are employed.

Increasingly, employers are heeding this advice, restructuring jobs, designing profit-sharing plans, or finding new ways of involving workers in decision-making.

SUGGESTIONS FOR GROUP SESSION

Opening

Begin this session by reading James 5:1–4, a passage that condemns greedy employers who pay their workers less than a fair wage. Although these employers may attain great wealth on earth, says James, the corrosion of their gold and silver will eventually testify against them.

For Discussion

1. Suppose you are the owner of a lumber operation, and you strongly suspect an employee named Fred of stealing from the yard. When you confront him, Fred denies any wrongdoing. As a Christian, can you in good conscience ask Fred to unlock the trunk of his car and allow you to examine its contents? Why or why not? Would it make a difference if you had received an anonymous note strongly suggesting that you ask Fred to unlock his trunk? Decide together what rights both the employer and the employee have in such a situation.
2. Suppose that Fred's case still remains unresolved. You're about ready to give up, but then you receive an anonymous note strongly suggesting that you drive to Fred's house and look in his garage and basement for your missing merchandise. You drive over to his house and discover that you can look through his garage and basement windows without ever setting foot on his property. So you do.

   Evaluate your actions in terms of your rights as an employer and Fred's right to privacy. How far may an employer go in prying into an employee's personal life? Where do we draw the line?
3. Because Pearl is strongly convinced that divorce is a great evil, she has a policy of never hiring a divorced person to work in her clothing store. One day Pearl happens to overhear a conversation among her employees and learns that one of her part-time clerks is in the process of going through a divorce. She

would like to terminate this employee but wonders if it would be ethical to do so under the circumstances. What advice would you give Pearl? Is it wrong for her to have such a policy in the first place?

4. In the spring of 1989 a large hospital in southwestern Michigan found it necessary to dismiss a substantial number of white-collar administrative employees. The workers were told in advance that they would be losing their jobs, but an outside consulting firm advised the hospital not to tell them the exact day they would be terminated. When they arrived at work on the morning of their last day, hospital management told employees to clear out their desks (under the watchful eye of an attendant). The consulting firm advised the hospital that it was particularly important that the departing employees have no last minute opportunity to empty files from the computer. One half hour after these employees discovered that this was their last day on the job, they were out the door.

   Evaluate the hospital's procedure.

5. In the fall of 1983 the Lockheed Corporation needed to hire several chemists for a job in Saudi Arabia. The Saudi government, with whom Lockheed had the contract, made it clear that no Jewish or female applicants would be acceptable. K. Bentley, director of Lockheed's science and application branch in Houston, was very uncomfortable with this stipulation. However, knowing that the company's important work in Saudi Arabia could not continue if he ignored the Saudi command, Bentley reluctantly posted job notices stating that female and Jewish applicants were not acceptable. Applying Garrett's third test, discuss whether Bentley had proportionate reasons for acting in the way he did.

6. Bill is an accountant who works for a small-town accounting firm deep in the Bible belt. Bill does excellent work, but he has a reputation for womanizing off the job. Most of the people who do business with the firm are devout people with traditional, old-fashioned values, and some have indicated to the partners of the firm that they are offended by Bill's lifestyle. The partners wonder what they should do. Is it their right to ask Bill to behave differently off the job, or is it Bill's right to conduct his life as he sees fit so long as it does not affect his performance on the job? Defend your choice.

7. Charles is a senior-level manager of a large corporation that has in recent years made considerable efforts to bring women into the management ranks. Charles has been with the firm for over twenty years and is greatly opposed to what the firm has been doing. He believes women lack the ability to do an effective job in

management and thinks that they should be confined to secretarial and clerical positions. Currently there are about a half dozen women in junior management positions, and Charles has decided simply to ignore them. When some of them are in the same room or speak to him, he refuses to even acknowledge their presence. To him they are nonentities.

Mention some forms of harassment that women commonly face in business careers. Why should or shouldn't Charles' treatment of the women in his corporation be described as a form of harassment?

Closing

You may want to end your session today by singing a hymn together. Especially appropriate is "What Does the Lord Require" (*Psalter Hymnal* 293, *Rejoice in the Lord* 176).

Then close by praying that those who supervise may be loving and trustful to those under their authority. Give thanks for Christian employers and pray that they might not lose sight of their workers' dignity and need to feel a sense of worth in their work.

RESOURCES FOR FURTHER STUDY

Engstom, Ted, and Edward Dayton. *The Christian Executive.* Waco, Texas: Word Publishing, 1979.

Hardy, Lee. *The Fabric of this World.* Grand Rapids, Michigan: Eerdmans, 1990.

Kreider, Carl. *The Christian Enterpreneur.* Scottsdale, Pennsylvania: Herald Press, 1980.

Velasquez, Manuel. *Business Ethics*, Second Edition. Englewood Cliffs, New Jersey: Prentice-Hall, 1988.

SESSION THREE

THE RESPONSIBLE EMPLOYEE

In January 1989, a Calvin College student from India made the following presentation in a course on business and engineering ethics:

> In January, 1986, after completing a course in automotive engineering, I began working as an apprentice on India's largest assembly line. The cars we turned out were reliable in almost every respect. The only problem was with the charging system. Almost every car produced was returned to the dealer within six weeks with a dead battery and invariably needed its alternator to be completely overhauled or even replaced. This problem not only blemished the company's name but also cost a great deal, since the necessary repairs were carried out under warranty at the company's expense.
>
> This flaw also caused considerable trouble and concern for the owners of these brand-new cars. After all, they had paid large sums of money over and above the cost of the car so that they might be pushed up on a seven-year waiting list to gain the right to purchase an automobile. They felt they deserved better than what they were getting.
>
> One day I was assigned the task of installing the infamous alternators on the cars. After a day's work, I asked the fore-

man's permission to take one of the alternators to my college where there was testing equipment. With the help of one of my professors, I learned why the alternators were giving people so much trouble. The coils were of inferior quality and failed to produce the required amount of current necessary to charge the battery. It was simply a matter of the manufacturer's failure to use lower-resistance, higher-quality wire.

A few days later I brought the alternator back to the factory and presented a written report of my findings to the foreman. He seemed interested in my findings but offered to do nothing about them. At first I was surprised at this. But I was even more surprised when he warned me in no uncertain terms not to try to take the matter any higher.

In spite of his warning, I took my report to the manager of purchasing. A few weeks later I was summoned to his office and told that if I didn't drop the matter immediately, I could expect to start looking for another job. It turned out that his superior, the director of purchasing, received large sums of money from the manufacturer of the alternators.

In a country where unemployment lingers at around 35 percent, I was not about to risk my position. So I stayed on my job, unhappy with myself and feeling quite helpless. I knew that no amount of whistle-blowing would accomplish anything. Had I taken the matter higher, the higher official I approached would only have cashed in on the deal. My only choice was to live with everyone else's unethical standards.

This case raises two significant issues regarding the responsibilities of an employee—issues involving bribery and whistle-blowing. Good ethics demand that an employee neither offer nor accept bribes and that an employee who becomes aware of serious ethical problems bring them to the attention of his superiors in the organization.

Anything for a Buck

Unfortunately the bribery described in this case is common in nearly every culture. In the February 1977 issue of *Business Horizons* Jack Kaikati observes,

> Almost every country has a name for it—"la mordita" in Latin America, "baksheesh" in the Middle East, "bustarella" in Italy, "hai yo" or "hung Pao" in Hong Kong, "dash" in some parts of Africa, "pot de vin" in France and "schmiergelder" in Ger-

many. Thus, no country has developed an immunity to bribery.

And that includes Canada and the United States. Bribery has infiltrated North American business in many subtle ways. All too typical is an incident reported in November, 1983, by *Business Week*. An accountant was asked to prepare a "business ethics" report for the Board of Directors of 7-11 Stores. His report made no mention of evidence he had uncovered of a manager that had attempted to bribe New York tax officials. When asked why his report neglected to mention this evidence, he replied that it did not seem important enough to be worth mentioning. To many in our culture the offer of a bribe does not seem like a wrongdoing of any particular significance.

Bribery is unethical because it disrupts the orderly course of business and gives an unfair advantage to the person offering the bribe. However, as pointed out earlier, it is also unethical because it strikes at the dignity of the person to whom the bribe is offered, tempting the person to compromise his or her own moral integrity. Seen in this light, the offer of a bribe seems to qualify as a major evil, something that is totally unjustifiable for a Christian to knowingly offer or accept.

Extortion, another evil present in the business world, differs from bribery in two major ways. First, while bribery is initiated by the person offering a payment or favor, extortion is initiated by a person seeking a payment or favor. Second, the person who is offered a bribe can freely choose to accept or reject the offer. But extortion involves an element of coercion, or blackmail. The victim knows the penalty for failure to make payment to or perform a favor for the person who demands it.

In spite of the differences between bribery and extortion, both are major evils and both can be present in forms so subtle that they are scarcely detectable. Because borderline cases of extortion and bribery are common in the way many people do business, it is important for Christians in business to be aware of the perils of these practices and to avoid placing themselves in compromising positions.

The Cost of Whistle-Blowing

The case of the defective alternators also raises the issue of whistle-blowing. There are times when employees become aware of problems that need to be brought to the attention of their employers, and, generally speaking, it is their moral responsibility to do so. In the case of the defective alternators, submitting the written report to the supervisors was the right thing to do.

Of course, problems arise when one's employer or supervisor refuses to do anything about what is an obvious ethical problem. A classic instance of this situation occurred during the construction of the Bay Area Rapid Transit system in the San Francisco area. Three engineers questioned the safety of certain equipment, including an Automatic Train Control System being built by the Westinghouse Corporation. The engineers communicated their reservations to their superiors but received no response. Several days after they went to the Bay Area Rapid Transit board of directors with their grievances, all three were fired.

In an out-of-court settlement, each won $25,000. But it took from eight to fifteen months for them to find suitable jobs elsewhere, and throughout the process they experienced a great deal of emotional stress. Whistle-blowing can be expensive.

Another well-known case involved an employee of a major airline. Dan Gellert had been a pilot with Eastern Airlines for over twenty-five years when he became aware of a serious defect in the auto-pilot mechanism of the Lockheed 1011 aircraft. Through working with a flight simulator, Gellert discovered that about ninety seconds before reaching ground level the auto-pilot would disengage without warning. When Gellert reported the problem to management, he was told that they would look into it. "You'd better before we kill a bunch of people," Gellert replied. Four months later, on December 29, 1972, that is exactly what happened. An Eastern Airlines 1011 crashed, killing 103 persons, and Gellert was convinced that the auto-pilot mechanism was to blame.

Again, Gellert sent a memorandum to Eastern officials, this time to the top three people in the company, and again his superiors made no attempt to correct the problem. After Gellert attempted to take the matter to the Airline Pilots Association and National Transportation Safety Board, he found that he had been demoted to a copilot. A short time later he was grounded. He spent seven months going through the company's grievance procedure before he was allowed to fly again in 1974.

In 1975 Gellert's attorney filed suit against Eastern airlines, and in 1977 Gellert was grounded again. When the case finally went to trial, the judge awarded Gellert $1,600,000. But the intervening five years had been something of a nightmare. Gellert had never wanted to be a whistle-blower, but he claims that his conscience allowed him no other choice.

Alleged instances of penalizing those who blow the whistle have also been reported by employees and former employees of U.S. government agencies. In 1975 the U.S. Senate held hearings on such abuses by these agencies. A worker for the Office of Economic Opportunities testified that he was fired after reporting arbitrary expenditures of day-care funds. Two women employed in the Indian Health Services lost their jobs after sending a letter to President Nixon about the mistreatment of patients in an Indian hospital. And an employee of the Department of Health, Education, and Welfare was penalized after she began raising questions about possible discriminatory practices in the hiring of agency employees.

Critics of whistle-blowing claim it is disruptive to business. James M. Roche, a former president of General Motors, put it this way:

> Some critics are now busy eroding another support of free enterprise—the loyalty of a management team, with its unifying values of cooperative work. Some of the enemies of business now encourage an employee to be disloyal to the enterprise. They want to create suspicion and disharmony, and pry into the proprietary interests of business. However this is labelled—industrial espionage, whistle-blowing, or professional responsibility—it is another tactic for spreading disunity and creating conflict.

Surely Roche is mistaken to characterize the whistle-blower as one who intends to be disruptive. Someone who reports serious problems to his or her employer is practicing good ethics. On the other hand, an employee ought not ordinarily report a problem publicly without first informing internal authorities. For example, Dan Gellert brought his findings about the auto-pilot problems to the Airline Pilots Association and National Transportation Safety Board only after first discussing these problems with the management of Eastern Airlines.

Do Wrong or Else

Sometimes employees, such as the college student installing the alternators, find that they themselves are being asked to contribute to the very problem that needs to be remedied. Dr. Grace Pierce, an employee of the Ortho Pharmaceutical Corporation, was assigned the task of developing a certain drug. It was her opinion that the drug she was asked to develop carried carcinogenic risks for consumers. However, she claims that management exerted pressures on her to continue developing the drug, insisting that it was perfectly legal. Pierce found herself forced to either proceed with the drug's development or leave the firm. Eventually she left the firm in the conviction that it was the only ethical thing to do.

Being asked to cooperate in wrongdoing is one of the toughest predicaments an employee can experience. David Ewing tells of a case in which a secretary was asked by her boss to tape telephone calls with clients. She believed that these clients should be told that the calls were being taped, and she refused to tape the calls if they were not informed. For refusing, she lost her job. She went to court in an effort to regain her job, but the court refused her request for reinstatement.

In most cases it is an employee's moral responsibility to refuse to cooperate in what appears to be wrongdoing, but there are situations in which one's moral responsibility might be unclear. Thomas Garrett describes a situation in which a secretary is asked to type up padded expense accounts for her boss. She knows that there is nothing she can do to stop this evil and that she will lose her job if she speaks out about the matter. But although her silence is a form of cooperation in evil, Garrett believes that her actions do not violate his five tests. Hence it is ethically permissible for her to type the documents. Of course, what is ethically permissible is not necessarily ethically praiseworthy, and in situations of this nature a Christian might wish to strive for more than that which is barely permissible.

Keeping It Confidential

An employee's responsibilities sometimes extend beyond the time of his or her employment. When taking a job with a competitor of one's former employer, for example, an employee may be asked not to divulge trade secrets to the new employer. One's former employer has the right to expect that such information remain secret.

Donald Wohlgemuth, a general manager for B.F. Goodrich, had access to secret technology in the firm's manufacture of space suits for the government. He left B.F. Goodrich to take a job with International Latex, a B.F. Goodrich competitor, at a considerably higher salary. One of the departments he was assigned to manage engaged in the manufacture of space suits. B.F. Goodrich went to court in an attempt to prevent Wohlgemuth from using the information and skills he acquired at Goodrich in his new position at International Latex. The Ohio Court of Appeals ruled that Wohlgemuth was free to make use of the skills he acquired at B.F. Goodrich in his new position. But the court also imposed an injunction, restraining him from disclosing any of B.F. Goodrich's trade secrets to International Latex.

In modern business organizations the value of information is increasingly significant, and hence there is an increasing need to think about the ethics of secrecy in business. Thomas Garrett distinguishes three types of secrets relevant to the business enterprise.

First is the *natural secret*, a secret which by its very nature will cause harm if it is revealed. For example, a supervisor with access to secret personnel files learned that one of her workers was an ex-convict. Obviously, she had a moral obligation not to exploit this information at the employee's expense.

Second is the *promised secret.* When employees promise to keep business and trade matters secret, they have a moral obligation to do so. Moreover, as we noted earlier, such promises can have the force of law.

Third is the *professional secret.* Certain professionals—such as clergy, physicians, lawyers, and accountants—can effectively carry out their work only if people trust them enough to reveal secrets to them. Their clients have the right to expect that their secrets will not be disclosed to others, and these professionals have the right to expect that they in turn will not be forced (by law enforcement authorities, for example) to relate these secrets to others.

But Garrett also admits that there are exceptional circumstances in all three categories in which one might have proportionate reasons for revealing that which is secret. For example, an employee might be justified in revealing company secrets in order to protect an innocent party from harm. And a minister might feel compelled to report an instance of child or spouse abuse to authorities in order to prevent further harm. However, we must exercise extreme caution in such situations, remembering that the dignity of the person involved may be at stake and keeping in mind Christ's injunction to love our neighbors as ourselves.

Daring to Be Honest

Equally important to knowing when to keep a secret is daring to tell the truth. Unfortunately, people in business are frequently advised that they can achieve true success only by being less than truthful. Consider, for instance, the advice offered by Albert Carr in a well-known *Harvard Business Review* article, "Is Business Bluffing Ethical?":

> To be a winner, a man must play to win. This does not mean that he must be ruthless, cruel, harsh, or treacherous. On the contrary, the better his reputation for integrity, honesty, and decency, the better his chances of victory will be in the long run. But from time to time every businessman, like every poker player, is offered a choice between certain loss or bluffing within the legal rules of the game. If he is not resigned to losing, if he wants to rise in the company and industry, then in such a crisis he will bluff—and bluff hard.
>
> *(January-February, 1968, p. 153)*

It is not illegal to bluff in business, just as it is not illegal to bluff in poker, and Carr believes one who does not engage in bluffing might as well be resigned to losing. No doubt there are circumstances in which bluffing in business is morally permissible and even praiseworthy. But what is disturbing about Carr's advice is the implication that there is no room in the world of business for a perfectly truthful person. One must play to win in the world of business, and a person who prefers not to engage in the game of bluffing is written off as faint of heart.

The business world's expectations of its employees has changed drastically in modern times. David Ewing, in his book *Freedom Inside the Organization* (New York: E.P. Dutton, Inc., 1977, p. 120), illustrates this point by way of a sign posted in a New York carriage shop in 1878:

> It is expected that each employee shall participate in the activities of the church and continue liberally in the Lord's work . . . . All employees are expected to be in bed by 10:00 P.M. Except: Each male employee may be given one evening a week for courting purposes.

Today it is inconceivable to think of church attendance and early bedtime as among the responsibilities of employees. These have been replaced by an entirely different set of expectations. And if Albert Carr is correct, one of these expectations is that an employee will do whatever it takes to be a winner. To many employers traditional values, such as being completely truthful, are better suited to the mentality of a bygone era. Those who hire all too often look for aggressive individuals with a fierce desire to win—men and women who have the killer instinct.

Fortunately, many Christians are resisting these expectations and proving that people can be successful in business without making compromises. In the long run a commitment to good values usually contributes to success, and placing a high premium on hiring those with a killer instinct can turn out to be a self-defeating strategy.

The Christian business community should do their best to serve as a role model for those entering business careers, helping them counter the pressures to conform. Good values have as legitimate a place in business as they do in any other area of our lives.

Honoring Your Employer

One final area of employee responsibility involves respect for the reputation of one's employer or the firm with which one is employed.

An employee should refrain from causing intentional damage to the firm's reputation. In some cases firms have terminated employees who have violated this responsibility, and courts have upheld the firm's right to do so.

One unusual case involved Louis V. McIntire, an employee of the Du Pont Corporation. McIntire, a technical employee for this large corporation, authored a novel about a "Marmaduke Glumm," a man who worked for a company bearing a strong resemblance to Du Pont. In the novel, Glumm is the victim of what is clearly corporate mismanagement, and he makes a strong case for the unionization of technical workers.

McIntire had a good record of fifteen years with Du Pont, but he was let go when the novel came to the attention of the Du Pont management. McIntire went to court, arguing that his right to free speech had been violated. But his claim was dismissed. Evidently the law recognizes that there are limits to the extent that one is allowed to speak out about one's employer. Employees have both a moral and a legal responsibility not to tarnish the reputation of the firms where they are employed.

SUGGESTIONS FOR GROUP SESSION

Opening

Read 2 Timothy 2:14-16, a passage that speaks of an employee's responsibility to be truthful. Here, the employee is instructed in all things to do his or her best to be presentable to God. Also, read and refer to the first part of section 51 of *Our World Belongs to God,* a Contemporary Testimony:

In our work, even in dull routine
we hear the call to serve our Lord.
We must work for more than wages,
and manage for more than profit,
so that mutual respect
and the just use of goods and skills
may shape the work place,
and so that, while we earn or profit,
useful products and services may result.

For Discussion

1. Your job involves a great deal of out-of-town travel, and your absence places a strain on your marriage. Your spouse would love to accompany you on your travels, but it appears to be financially unfeasible. Then you discover that you can take your

spouse along by flying tourist instead of first-class, staying in a less expensive hotel, and so forth. You find that the bills you present to your company are about the same as they were before. You haven't actually received permission from your superior to take your spouse along; but you feel that your job performance suffers when you are experiencing marital difficulties, and that therefore it is in the company's best interests for your spouse to accompany you. Besides, your company ought to be willing to keep your marriage intact.

Have you done anything unethical? If so, what? Why do or don't you have proportionate reasons for engaging in this deception? Can you think of any reasons why your superior might object to this practice?

2. People in North America frequently express shock at the bribery practiced in other nations of the world. This attitude has puzzled visitors from other nations who find what they consider to be widespread bribery in North American society in the form of offering "tips," "honoraria," or "gratuities" to those from whom one wants an unspoken favor. Thus, North Americans are widely regarded as hypocritical in their condemnation of bribery in other nations.

   Where exactly would you draw the line between a bribe and a gratuity? Is it a form of bribery to offer a member of a legislative body a huge honorarium for delivering a short speech to members of a special interest group? Is it a form of bribery to tip the head server in a restaurant in hopes of being seated at a choice table? Defend your position.

3. Joe is a purchasing agent for a large auto parts wholesaler. Salespeople are constantly trying to stay on his good side, and Joe is uneasy about accepting gifts from them. He regularly turns down offers for weekend vacation trips and returns lavish gifts that salespeople shower him with. These strike him as forms of bribery. But Joe is less sure what to do about smaller gifts, such as tickets to ball games or bottles of liquor at Christmas.

   Should he return these smaller "favors" as well or does he have a proportionate reason for accepting them? When salespeople insist on picking up the lunch tab, for example, may Joe allow them to? As a Christian, Joe wants to do what is right and to set a good example for others. What advice would you give him?

4. You are a server in a fairly nice restaurant. Over the course of time you begin to recognize certain regular customers. Some consistently leave good tips, and some consistently leave modest or poor tips. You make no effort to provide good service to those in the latter category. After serving their food, you deliberately neglect to return to see if they require more service. Once in

a while, though, you feel guilty about your behavior. Could your actions be described as a mild form of extortion? To satisfy Garrett's fifth test, try to come up with a reasonable alternative to the way you treat these customers.

5. In *The Ethics of Management* (p. 19), Professor Hosmer quotes a former student as follows:

> There are executives in our company who will select a flight based upon the frequent-flyer benefits, not upon the cost to the company or the time spent in the air. The man for whom I work is probably the greatest offender; he gets me and others, when we fly, to use his card so that he accumulates the mileage—and the freebies.
>
> Our company has a corporate code of conduct. The chairman gets us all together once a year and talks about the high standards of [name of the company], yet here is an executive ripping everybody off, and nobody cares. In fact, the chairman probably approves; he always uses one of the corporate jets for his own vacation travel.

   What responsibilities has this executive failed to fulfill or exercise? Have you observed similar practices in a business organization? If so, describe them for the group.

6. Discuss Garrett's example of the secretary who is asked to type padded expense accounts for her boss. Do you agree with Garrett that what she is doing is not necessarily unethical? Explain. Have you ever worked for an employer who asked you to cooperate in something that you knew was wrong? If so, how did you handle the situation?

Closing

As a group, you may want to sing the hymn "What Does the Lord Require" as you did last week.

Then close with prayer, asking for the wisdom and insight to know one's responsibilities as an employee. Remember any specific examples of problems mentioned, and pray for each other by name. Ask God to give each member of the group the grace to exercise his or her responsibilities as an employee in a way that is sensitive to both employer and fellow employees.

RESOURCES FOR FURTHER STUDY

Carr, Albert Z. "Is Business Bluffing Ethical?" *Harvard Business Review*, January-February, 1968, p. 143.

Smedes, Lewis. "Business Ethics—Standards and Strategies," *Reformed Journal*, January, 1981, p. 6.

Van de Riet, Garrett. "The Christian in Business Administration," *The Banner*, September 1, 1961, p. 15.

Yates, Jere E. "Business Ethics: A Christian Perspective," *Mission Journal*, June, 1982, p. 11.

SESSION FOUR

CONSUMER RIGHTS

In 1985, a federal suit charged that eight record companies conspired to fix, raise, and maintain the price of records and tapes. According to an article in the *Wall Street Journal* in April, 1985, three record companies agreed to pay a total of $11.2 million to settle the suit. RCA agreed to pay $4.9 million, Polygram $3.5 million, and Capital-EMI $2.8 million. Earlier CBS and MCA had settled for $4.3 million and $1.7 million, respectively.

In another government suit Binney & Smith, Inc. and Milton Bradley Co. were charged with fixing the price of art supplies at unnaturally high levels. Binney & Smith, maker of Crayola Crayons, was charged by the Federal Trade Commission with agreeing with some of its competitors to set high prices on chalk, crayons, water-colors, and tempera paints. Binney & Smith and Milton Bradley agreed to pay $1.2 million to school systems across the country.

This session deals with the rights of consumers. People have long been aware that the rights of consumers need to be protected. The Code of Hammurabi, written almost 4,000 years ago, emphasizes that merchants have the responsibility to deal fairly with consumers and to be concerned with product safety. In the Judeo-Christian tradition there has been a parallel concern for the rights of buyers (Lev. 19:35–36, Amos 8:5–6). However, through long periods of history, little was done to promote consumer rights and people were willing to live by the slogan, "Let the buyer beware."

In contemporary North American society there is a great deal of awareness of consumer rights, and product liability law has shifted from a "buyer beware" perspective to "let the seller beware" emphasis. More than ever before, consumers are insisting upon their rights. And, more than ever before, companies are being forced to take seriously their responsibility to deal fairly with consumers and to produce safe, quality products.

Companies Who Resist

The companies cited in the opening examples are not the exception. Many corporations have failed to take their responsibilities to the consumer seriously.

In March, 1984, criminal charges were brought against National Semiconductor for improper testing of computer chips for a defense contract, falsification of test reports, and lying to government officials about the testing of computer parts for military contractors. Sources reported that officials at National actually approved the formation of teams of employees who worked full-time for weeks fabricating testing-verification documents to be reviewed by Defense Department officials.

One employee made the following statement:

> I'd say that over 100 employees had to know. To say that dozens participated would be a very conservative estimate . . . Just about everybody in production control knew about it who had been there for six months . . . . Yeah, we did make it up. There was a lot of documentation I personally dummied up . . . . When I realized how deeply things were being falsified, I just couldn't believe it.

Another outrageous example of disregard for the rights of consumers concerns the infamous "500" steel-belted radial tires manufactured by the Firestone Tire and Rubber Company. In January, 1977, after a legislative subcommittee found that these tires had been associated with 15 deaths and 31 injuries, Firestone announced that it had discontinued manufacture of the tire. However, in 1978 the subcommittee discovered to its astonishment that, despite the announcement, Firestone had quietly continued manufacture of the tire.

Insurance companies are another group often suspected of being less than fair to consumers. Senator Daniel Patrick Moynihan has charged that insurance companies regularly engage in what he calls "unethical" practices toward their policyholders. According to Moynihan, insurance agents often use outdated actuarial tables in order to charge unfairly high premiums. They habitually create delays in the hearings of suits against them in a calculated effort to wear down those bringing the suits and make a cheap settlement more likely. In addition, Moynihan charges that insurance companies have often employed shrewd strategies that are highly discriminatory toward certain minority groups.

Situations like these have led to the formation of consumer-rights groups. Advocates of these groups have been actively lobbying for legislation to protect consumers from over-priced, inferior quality, or dangerous goods and services. Partly as a result of these efforts, it has become easier to prosecute firms producing such goods and services.

Early in the twentieth century a consumer could prosecute a retailer for selling goods causing death or injury, but one could not prosecute the manufacturer of these goods. However, in 1916 a man named Donald MacPherson brought suit against the Buick Motor Company for injuries caused by the loss of a wheel on his new Buick. MacPherson won the case, and ever since that time the firms themselves have been considered legally responsible for their products.

Justice in Jingles

Firms are also responsible for the manner in which they promote their products. Good ethics demands advertising that does not mislead potential consumers. In a 1944 decision the United States Supreme Court recommended "a form of advertising clear enough so that, in the words of the prophet Isaiah, 'wayfaring men, though fools, shall not err therein.' "

There is considerable disagreement over what constitutes misleading or deceptive forms of advertising. Some insist that exaggeration is just as acceptable in advertising as it is in other segments of life, that one should more or less expect a certain degree of exaggeration in advertising. As one commentator recently put it,

> No sane American would think that literally everybody is 'talking about the new Starfire' or that a woman wearing a Distinction foundation garment becomes so beautiful that her sisters literally want to kill her.

Most people also are fully aware that the exaggerated claims of competing products cannot all be true:

1. "For speed and strength of relief, Bayer is unsurpassed by any other product tested, including the so-called 'extra-strength' one that claims to be 50% stronger."

2. "Tablet for tablet, 50% stronger than aspirin" (Excedrin).
3. "Bufferin delivers twice as much pain reliever twice as fast as aspirin."
4. "Anacin is strongest in the pain relievers doctors recommend most."

One would be considered foolish to take these claims seriously and to worry about reconciling them with one another.

Others argue that we should have higher expectations about truthfulness in advertising and that many of the standard practices of those producing advertising for television are ethically problematic. For example, hot wine is frequently used in commercials for coffee, since it has a more desirable appearance on camera. For similar reasons mashed potatoes are sometimes used in ice cream commercials. And in ads for Campbell's vegetable soup, clear glass marbles are strategically positioned in the bowl to enhance the appearance of solidity. Some feel that practices such as these are mild forms of deception and should not be used.

In a variety of cases the Federal Trade Commission has stepped in to prevent consumers from being deceived. For example, in one well-known case a number of years ago, Colgate-Palmolive ran an ad for its Rapid Shaving Cream in which Rapid Shave was being used to shave sandpaper ("Apply, soak, and off in a stroke"). The so-called sandpaper was actually plexiglass, and the United States Supreme Court ruled in favor of the Federal Trade Commission that the ad was deceptive.

Colgate-Palmolive argued in its defense that Rapid Shave really can be used to shave sandpaper. Unfortunately, the sandpaper must be soaked in Rapid Shave for eighty minutes before it can be shaved, and viewers of the ad were not informed of the eighty-minute wait. Because, said the court, Colgate-Palmolive was using the ad to falsely establish additional proof of the quality of the product, they were involved in deceptive and unfair advertising.

Since the Colgate-Palmolive decision, the Federal Trade Commission has actively challenged the claims made on behalf of many products. Goodyear Tire has boasted that its Double-Eagle Polysteel Tires can be driven over ax blades without suffering damage, and Sears, Roebuck and Company has claimed that its steel-belted radial tires can be driven 60,000 to 101,000 miles. In both instances the Federal Trade Commission requested proof. Likewise, the Commission challenged General Motors' claim that its Vega's ground beams provide more side-impact collision protection than those of any comparable compact car and Chrysler's claim that its electronic system never needs tuning.

Beyond Deception

Questions about the ethics of advertising go beyond the issue of deception. In recent years several large cigarette manufacturers have stepped up their efforts to increase sales in Third World countries. Cigarette sales in North America have been declining for over a decade due to concerns over health, and Third World countries offer the promise of compensating for these declining sales. Consequently, massive advertising campaigns have been initiated in these nations.

According to LaRue Hosmer, these advertising campaigns usually depict prosperous members of the dominant racial group of the country smoking cigarettes in enviable surroundings. Cigarettes have been made available in local shops and markets, and since they're sold singly rather than by the pack, many people can afford them. Thus, even though sales in North America and Western Europe have declined dramatically, companies such as Philip Morris have managed to increase overall sales by 5 per cent for the past five years. Incredibly, Philip Morris now sells cigarettes in one hundred seventy countries.

Surely situations of this type ought to be of concern to Christians. A number of years ago large numbers of Christians protested, largely for health-related reasons, the marketing practices of firms selling infant formula in Third World nations. Given what is now known about the effects of cigarette smoking, it would be well for concerned Christians to consider taking a similar stance on the marketing practices of these cigarette manufacturers.

Critics have expressed related concerns about Union Carbide's role in the Bhopal disaster of December 2, 1984. On that date a poisonous leak of methyl isocyanate gas from the Union Carbide plant in Bhopal, India, led to the deaths of two thousand people and injuries to about two hundred thousand others. Authorities claim that Union Carbide should never have introduced such a dangerous and complex modern pesticide technology into a nation with a highly unskilled workforce and a significant illiterate population. Although Union Carbide's actions were not so deliberately and knowingly harmful as are those of the cigarette companies, one can make a strong case that the actions of both fail to satisfy the conditions of Garrett's fourth test.

It is abundantly clear from the Scriptures that human life is of immeasurable value (Gen. 1:27, Ps. 8:5-6, Ps. 139:13-14), and from this we can imply that firms have a responsibility of highest proportions to take precautions against anything that threatens life. The Ford Motor Company has been roundly criticized for its decision not to install certain safety devices on its Pinto during the model years of the early 1970s. A technological improvement costing $11 per car would have prevented its gas tanks from rupturing so easily, but Ford refused to install the device. This decision appears to have led to several deaths.

However, one prominent journalist, Mark Dowie, believes that other firms deserve the same condemnation:

> Unfortunately, the Pinto is not an isolated case of corporate malpractice in the auto industry. Neither is Ford a lone sinner. There probably isn't a car on the road without a safety hazard known to its manufacturer . . . . Furthermore, cost-valuing human life is not used by Ford alone. Ford was just the only company careless enough to let such an embarrassing calculation slip into public records. The process of willfully trading lives for profits is built into corporate capitalism. Commodore Vanderbilt publicly scorned George Westinghouse and his "foolish" air brakes while people died by the hundreds in accidents on Vanderbilt's railroads.
>
> —*"Pinto Madness",* Mother Jones, *September-October, 1977, p. 32*

In a day and age of consumer-rights activism, one might hope that attitudes such as Commodore Vanderbilt's would have become relics of another era. Unfortunately, there is plenty of evidence that this is not the case. A typical example involves the Paydozer's earth-moving machine, which has no provision for rear view. Even though operators of these machines have sometimes backed over and killed people who were standing behind them, the company has refused to acknowledge any responsibility for the problem.

Court Crackdowns

Courts of law have become increasingly less tolerant toward such callous disregard for the life and safety of human beings. A few years ago Winthrop Laboratories marketed a painkiller which they advertised as "nonaddictive." When a patient became addicted to the drug and died from an overdose, a court ruled that because Winthrop Laboratories had expressly stated that the drug was nonaddictive, the company was to be held liable for the patient's death.

Indeed, some would argue that courts have become too hard on manufacturers—that the pendulum has swung too far to the opposite extreme.

A vacuum cleaner designed to be used in a standard 115 volt outlet was plugged into a 220 volt circuit, and the machine blew up. The manufacturer argued that the machine was equipped with a label clearly stating that the vacuum was to be plugged into a 115 volt outlet. Nevertheless, the Kentucky Court of Appeals argued that the manufacturer was responsible for what happened since it failed to state that plugging the machine into a higher voltage outlet would be highly dangerous. (The court drew an analogy between the vacuum cleaner label and a "Keep off the grass" sign posted in an area infested with deadly snakes.)

It could be argued that unreasonable demands are sometimes made on firms that are making an honest effort to produce quality goods which are safe to their users. And it could be argued that governmental agencies in charge of overseeing these matters have sometimes harassed these firms and burdened them with unfair, nitpicking regulations. But it is important to remember that in the absence of regulations, it would be all too easy for many people in management to slip back into the mindset of Commodore Vanderbilt. In the absence of consumer-rights protection, the temptation to maximize profits could blind one to the need to assign the health and safety of the consumer the highest priority.

Working for Consumer Good

It would be naive to assume that Christians in business are immune from such temptations or that Christians never exploit the weak-willed or those with irrational desires. Thomas Garrett cautions Christians in business to be careful not to take advantage of the grief-stricken making funeral arrangements, young people buying an engagement ring, parents making wedding arrangements, or people borrowing money for medical expenses. People in these situations can be particularly vulnerable to unscrupulous sales tactics. Recent immigrants, illegal aliens, or those with a poor grasp of English are also easy prey. Garrett recalls seeing a brand-new set of Encyclopedia Brittanica in the home of people who could neither read nor speak English. No doubt other examples of unethical sales techniques come readily to the minds of many readers.

It's important that Christians adopt a particularly high standard of ethics in dealing with the weak willed or those with irrational desires, for taking advantage of such people is an affront to the dignity of the individual. It is good business, as well as good ethics, to honor the dignity of one's customers or potential customers.

An article by David Aaker and George Day in the *Harvard Business Review* notes that some large corporations have begun thinking of marketing more in terms of focusing on long-run consumer interests and solving social problems than in terms of short-run profits. They cite Whirlpool as a pioneer in developing a program of this type, and they believe that this corporation's comprehensive consumer-oriented program has been a success by all conventional measures. Thus, some firms are beginning to think in terms of producing goods and services that can truly contribute to the quality of life for all of society.

Perhaps this is a hopeful sign of things to come. Surely it is an approach which is based upon treating potential consumers as dignified human beings with rights and respectability rather than as suckers to be taken advantage of.

Unfortunately, many firms seem intent upon taking advantage of consumers in every way they can. All too typical are the sales practices of Pacific Bell Telephone Company. A report by the Pacific Utilities Commission of California stated that service representatives of Pacific Bell made a point of quoting a fee for new telephone service which included several expensive optional features. The basic service was available at a much lower monthly fee, but their hope was to dupe new customers into buying the expensive options.

One sales representative described the situation as follows:

> I'm told to tell the customer, "You will get unlimited local calling, Touchtone service, our four custom-calling services . . . and it's only $22.20 per month." Most customers will say, "That's fine." It really isn't a bad deal, but how many people know they don't have to buy all those things, that they can get basic service for $9.95? The company says, "People should be intelligent enough to ask; why should it be PacBell's job to tell them?" People who don't speak English well, they end up with those services.
>
> —*Quoted in Manuel Velasquez,* Business Ethics, *Englewood Cliffs, New Jersey: Prentice-Hall, 1988, p. 272*

Things have come a long way from the days of "let the buyer beware" and reckless disregard for the safety and health of consumers typified by Commodore Vanderbilt. No doubt Christians in the business community have contributed to this new climate. But the examples cited in this lesson illustrate some of the enormous challenges that remain for those who are truly concerned about producing goods and services that will improve the quality of life.

SUGGESTIONS FOR GROUP SESSION

Opening

Read Proverbs 21:6–8,15 together. Talk about the implications of this passage for a merchant who amasses a fortune (or even makes a small profit) through dishonesty. Then open with prayer, asking for God's presence in your discussion and for God's help in leading you to make ethical choices that benefit rather than harm humanity.

For Discussion

1. The Supreme Court took a tolerant attitude toward advertisers who used "minor deceptions" in their ads, claiming that such deceptions were permissible as long as they did not establish additional proof for the quality of the product.

   Evaluate the court's ruling. How might it apply to an advertiser who used hot wine to depict hot coffee or mashed potatoes to depict ice cream? To the company who used clear glass marbles to make their soup look thicker? May a Christian participate in such deceptions? Why or why not?
2. In his book *Where the Law Ends*, Christopher Stone describes the marketing practices of the Holland Furnace Company a number of years ago.

   > Company representatives, claiming to be furnace inspectors, would offer homeowners a free safety insection. The representatives would then dismantle the furnace, declare it unsafe, and refuse to reassemble a device so deadly to its owners. Minutes later a salesperson from Holland Furnace would just happen to come calling at the door, and the homeowner would have an opportunity to discuss the purchase of a new furnace. Stone contends that these practices continued for some twenty years. Eventually the executives of Holland Furnace were held in contempt, and the president was sentenced to six months in prison.

   Think of some examples of how this type of marketing practice is used in more subtle forms today.
3. In 1978 the Food and Drug Administration required manufacturers of hair dyes containing the chemical 4-MMPD to carry the following label: "Contains an ingredient that can penetrate your skin and has been determined to cause cancer in laboratory animals." Most of the major hair dye manufacturers responded by reformulating their products so that they no longer contained 4-MMPD. Revlon's strategy was to replace this chemical with the ingredient 4-EMPD, which has an almost identical chemical structure. In this way the company was able to avoid printing a warning label on their products.

   Evaluate Revlon's decision. Did it conform to the letter of the law? To the spirit of the law? As a Christian, why would or wouldn't you have been comfortable making the decision made by the Revlon management? Applying Garrett's third test, could Revlon plausibly argue that it had proportionate reasons for its decision? Explain your answer.

4. Advertisers frequently claim that their ads serve consumers by providing them with useful information. However, in one study the people surveyed regarded only 5.8 percent of all ads informative—that is, "ads that you learn something from, that you are glad to know or know about . . . that help you in one way or another because of the information they provide."

   Together think of as many ads as you can that actually provide you as the consumer with useful information. What can you and members of your congregation do to promote better values in business? To critically analyze the advertisements that bombard us daily?

5. Blood Plasma International, a Florida firm, wasted no time arriving on the scene of a Nicaraguan earthquake disaster. To many the firm appeared to be an angel of mercy. However, when BPI began charging up to 150 times the amount they had paid for the blood, it became obvious that their motives were less than charitable.

   Were the actions of this firm morally objectionable? Why or why not? Give some other examples in which the victims of disastrous circumstances have been exploited by those seeking a quick profit.

6. As the owner of a small grocery store, you offer lottery tickets for sale. Some of your regular customers live well below the poverty line, yet they purchase lottery tickets in great numbers. You are concerned that money needed to feed their families is being squandered on these tickets.

   Should you refuse to sell tickets to such people? Is it wrong for Christians to become involved in the sale of lottery tickets in the first place? Defend your answer.

7. On February 26, 1985, the *Wall Street Journal* carried the following item:

   > It was a month before Christmas 1983, and Katherine Snow, an unmarried mother, needed money. Subsisting on a monthly income of only $423, Ms. Snow sought help from Thorp Finance Corp., Wisconsin's biggest consumer-loan company. Thorpe . . . agreed to lend Ms. Snow $126.72. But it also induced Ms. Snow to borrow $14.72 for credit life insurance, $73.44 for property insurance and $202 for term life insurance. Finally, for an additional $24.50, Ms. Snow became a member of the ITT Consumer Thrift Club, entitling her to discounts on consumer products . . . . Ms.

> Snow was a victim of "packing," a lucrative practice in which a lender adds payments for "optional" insurance and other products to the amount of the loan without the consumer's requesting them.

Evaluate this marketing practice. Which of Garrett's five tests would be relevant?

Closing

Pray that those who sell may have purity of heart and a desire to bring genuine benefits to society. Pray that they may resist the temptation to deceive or exploit.

RESOURCES FOR FURTHER STUDY

Schultze, Quentin. "Poets for Hire: The Ethics of Consumer Advertising," *Media Development*, 3, 1987, p. 2.

Stone, Christopher. *Where the Law Ends*. New York: Harper & Row, 1975.

SESSION FIVE

NO CORPORATION IS AN ISLAND

For many years a Japanese corporation named Chisso dumped waste materials containing significant quantities of mercury into the ocean. When the local residents ate fish poisoned with mercury, their bodies began to accumulate the substance. In time this contamination led to many grotesque and crippling birth defects.

Although Chisso was well aware that the mercury posed a serious danger to local residents, the corporation continued to dump its wastes into the ocean. The guidelines that the Japanese government had established for the emission levels of mercury were seriously inadequate. As a result, Chisso officials were secure in the knowledge that they were breaking no law.

Two of the previous sessions dealt with the responsibilities firms have—first to their employees and then to consumers. Nevertheless, more needs to be said about the responsibilities of firms and of the people managing them. As the scenario with Chisso illustrates, firms are also responsible for the safety and well being of the local community and for keeping the environment clean. In addition, firms and those who manage them have a variety of responsibilities to their shareholders, governmental agencies, their competitors, their dealers and suppliers, labor unions, and the public at large. This lesson will single out for discussion some pertinent issues that emerge from a consideration of these responsibilities.

Deciding Where the Buck Stops

Some people are uncomfortable with the idea that corporations have responsibilities; after all, corporations are not human beings. (In one famous legal opinion, a frustrated judge noted that they have "no pants to kick or soul to damn.")

Others, such as James McKie of the Brookings Institution, believe that business organizations have just *one* responsibility: to seek profit. According to McKie the pursuit of profit will in fact enhance public welfare, but firms should not consider it their responsibility to enhance the welfare of anything or anyone other than their own. Or, as University of Chicago economist Milton Friedman puts it,

> Few trends could so thoroughly undermine the very foundations of our free society as the acceptance by corporate officials of a social responsibility other than to make as much money for their stockholders as possible.
>
> —Capitalism and Freedom, *Chicago: University of Chicago Press, 1962, p. 13*

Sometimes Christians who are critical of a free-market economy speak as if the pursuit of profit is evil in whatever form it appears. Their ideal is usually a communal-style economy modeled along the lines of what is described in Acts 4. This is an extreme view and, Acts 4 notwithstanding, one will look in vain to find clear scriptural condemnation of the profit motive. On the other hand, it is also difficult to defend the other extreme, typified by McKie and Friedman.

A balanced view recognizes that a firm has diverse responsibilities and that the extremes of "profit only" or "no profit" are untenable. The views of McKie and Friedman treat concern for society and the environment as if it is of no direct concern to those who manage. And those who condemn the profit motive as wicked are insensitive to the firm's responsibilities toward its shareholders: surely shareholders have a right to expect that a firm will make efforts to be profitable.

Responsibilities to Shareholders

This last point deserves some explanation.

To begin with, shareholders have a right to expect that the company they have invested in will make profits and that some of these profits will be paid to them in the form of dividends. Today this right is almost taken for granted, but on some occasions shareholders have charged that firms have been unreasonably stingy in paying dividends. In one memorable 1919 court decision, Henry

Ford was ordered to increase dividends to shareholders of the Ford Motor Company.

On other occasions shareholders have attempted to prevent firms from giving to charity funds that might have been used to increase dividends. In the early 1960s Alice V. Gordon, a shareholder of the Standard Oil Company of New Jersey, formally challenged the company's practice of awarding cash grants to private colleges through its ESSO Education Foundation.

Mrs. Gordon remarked as follows:

> Your directors are giving millions of dollars of your corporation's money to charity. This seems wrong. Your company is supposedly run solely for the stockholders' benefit. . . . Many stockholders undoubtedly feel that charity begins at home. Others who can afford donations are certainly entitled to choose their beneficiaries. The current practice is especially reprehensible when one realizes that nearly ten million dollars have been given since 1955 to educational institutions, many of which now teach socialism and ridicule businessmen, savers, and investors.
>
> —*as quoted in* Cases in Business Ethics, *eds., Thomas Garrett and others, Englewood Cliffs, New Jersey: Prentice-Hall, 1968, p. 225*

In contrast, other stockholders have sometimes pressured firms to become *more* aware of their responsibilities to society. In 1970 a group organized by Ralph Nader bought shares of General Motors' common stock. The group arranged for a number of resolutions to appear on the annual stockholders' report. One called for establishing a corporate committee on social responsibility, and another proposed new publicly-oriented representatives to sit on the Board of Directors. Although these resolutions were easily defeated at the annual meeting, the widespread publicity of these proposals led to a great deal of public criticism of General Motors. The company eventually decided to establish a committee on social responsibility.

In another case, the Sisters of the Precious Blood, a group of Roman Catholic nuns who owned one thousand shares of Bristol-Myers stock, became alarmed over Bristol-Myers' marketing of infant formula in Third World nations. The nuns alleged that mothers were encouraged to use formula in place of breast-feeding, that many users of the product had access only to water with high bacteria levels, and that most users were too poor to continue purchasing the product in adequate quantities. Having abandoned breast-feeding, the mothers were forced to rely upon whatever meager quantities of the product they could afford. The result was widespread malnutrition. Eventually, in 1978, the sisters filed suit against Bristol-Myers, and the case was settled out-of-court: Bristol-Myers agreed to work with the nuns in helping to solve the problems created by their marketing practices in these nations.

It's easy to assume that a person must hold an influential management position in order to successfully promote Christian principles in the world of business. But this example of what the Sisters of the Precious Blood accomplished, along with similar accounts of other Christians who have used their position as shareholders to urge corporations to pull out of South Africa, serves as an important reminder that Christians with investments in business have both an opportunity and a responsibility to let their voices be heard.

Responsibilities to Organized Labor

A firm also has important responsibilities in its relationship with organized labor.

First of all, it's important that we recognize that unions have a right to exist. Without unions and the bilateral agreements they make possible between management and employees, workers in a variety of industries would be treated unjustly. It is true that labor unions have been guilty of certain abusive practices of their own (including, in some cases, collusion with management), but these should not blind one to their legitimacy and the considerable benefits, both material and immaterial, they bring to millions of people.

It is all too common for North American Christians who have been raised with a strong work ethic to develop a hostile and intolerant attitude toward organized labor; some were openly gleeful over the fate of organized labor during the 1980s. Former President Reagan's firing of the air traffic controllers seemed to signal a new era of anti-labor sentiment in North America. Many interpreted this action as a declaration of war on organized labor, some as an invitation to engage in union-busting activities. As a result, the influence of organized labor has been noticeably on the decline in recent years.

The truth is that organized labor was the victim of some significant injustices during the 1980s. For example, Continental Airlines went out of business and dissolved all of its union contracts, then came into existence again the next day as a new corporation with the same employees—now paid at non-union scale. Though Continental's actions were perfectly legal (at the time), it is hard to defend this company's behavior from an ethical point of view.

Such actions should be of great concern to Christians as together we work for justice and fairness in the marketplace. Christians who are members of labor unions can constitute a Christian presence—seeking to oppose abusive, wasteful, or inefficient practices. Christians in management can demonstrate an attitude of trust and concern toward their unionized employees and the organizations that represent them at the bargaining table. And Christians in general can seek to develop a more respectful and understanding attitude toward organized labor, recognizing it as an institution committed to protecting human beings from potential exploitation by business enterprises.

Responsibilities to Competitors

A firm also must understand and recognize the rights of its competitors. Casebooks are full of underhanded and deceitful practices calculated to harm one's competitors. While a great many laws have been enacted spelling out the limits of what can be tolerated in dealing with one's competitors, there is plenty of room within the limits of these laws for unethical practices.

First, it is always unethical by Garrett's first test to willfully seek to harm one's competitors. For example, it is always wrong to spread malicious gossip about a competitor's product or personnel, even when the actual facts are true. This is not to say that it is always wrong to harm one's competitors. A firm that develops a superior product or service will take over a greater share of the market, and that will harm competitors by reducing their profits. But, in and of itself, there is nothing unethical in bringing about this type of harm.

Sometimes it is even morally permissible to will harm to one's competitor for the sake of promoting a greater good. According to Garrett's third test, however, this behavior is morally permissible only if the proportionality requirement is satisfied. For example, a firm might make an attractive offer of employment to key personnel already working for a competitor. Such offers are not unethical if they are motivated not by a desire to harm the competitor (to acquire trade secrets, for instance) but rather by the desire to benefit from the talents of these key employees. Here, as in all areas that fall under the scope of Garrett's third test, Christians should proceed with caution and should be mindful of Christ's admonition to love one's neighbor as oneself.

Responsibilities to Government

A firm's responsibilities to governments and governmental agencies are, on the face of things, quite straightforward: everything must be done within the limits of the law. Unfortunately, often it is not clear whether a particular course of conduct is legal or illegal. On these occasions one's decision is largely a matter of ethics. Sometimes, as in the Chisso example, it is clear that the law is inadequate—that it fails to prohibit practices that are clearly unethical. In these situations, good ethics dictate restraint in taking advantage of loopholes in the law.

In 1977, the United States Congress passed the Foreign Corrupt Practices Act. Among other things, this legislation prohibits firms from bribing officials in overseas countries while conducting business in these nations. Prior to the passage of this legislation, such bribery was common among North American firms attempting to find new foreign markets. These firms argued that bribery was a necessary part of doing business in many of these countries, and when in Rome one must do as the Romans do.

Nevertheless, many people sensed that there was something morally problematic in these business practices—especially when the press reported shocking cases of multi-million dollar bribes. In 1970 the Gulf Corporation paid three million dollars to Korea's ruling party. In a Senate investigation, Bob R. Dorsey, Gulf's chairman, simply stated that the payoff was necessary to secure the continued favor of the regime. In 1975 the Lockheed Corporation admitted that it had made under-the-table payments of about 22 million dollars to a number of overseas officials. Lockheed's president, Carl Kotchian, personally traveled to Japan with suitcases stuffed with cash and paid 3.2 million dollars to Japanese officials to ensure the sale of its L-1011 Tri-Star jet liners. (The Lockheed situation was particularly irritating to U.S. taxpayers since the company had been on the brink of bankruptcy in 1971 and had asked Congress to bail it out with a guaranteed loan.) Altogether, over four hundred American companies made bribes to foreign officials of over 300 million dollars prior to 1977.

The passage of the Foreign Corrupt Practices Act was significant. In effect, it conveyed the message that there are moral limits to what a company can do when dealing with those of other nations or cultures. No longer can a corporation excuse itself by saying they are simply doing what is required by the practices of another culture. If it is wrong to offer or accept bribes in our own culture, it is likewise wrong to offer or accept bribes when dealing with those of another culture. Our standards of conduct must not be compromised—no matter whom we are dealing with.

Stricter guidelines may also be needed to prevent corporations from dishonest dealings with governmental agencies, particularly those connected with defense. B.F. Goodrich was so eager to obtain an Air Force contract to develop brake assemblies that its management instructed that the contract be acquired "at all costs." The contract was acquired, but only after the engineering department at B.F. Goodrich doctored and falsified reports of numerous tests over a period of several months. When Air Force A7D planes equipped with the new brake assemblies were ceremoniously displayed at Edwards Air Force base, the brakes failed repeatedly. During one landing a brake actually welded shut, sending the plane skidding a quarter mile before it finally stopped.

How could such a thing have happened at B.F. Goodrich? Thomas Donaldson describes the situation as follows:

> The decision to go after the Air Force brake contract "at all costs" was made by the corporate hierarchy and laid unceremoniously at the door of the engineering department. No communication occurred between the two which might have clarified the meaning of the "at all costs" proviso. Upper management had no idea how its directives were being interpreted and was not informed that the brakes were faulty until the scandal broke . . . . At lower levels, individuals were reluctant to blow the whistle because they saw their obligation as simply doing their jobs and "following the rules."
>
> The official supervisor for the engineering department turned a deaf ear to complaints. Not having an engineering degree himself, he was compelled, he said, to trust the professional skills of the designer.
>
> —Corporations and Morality, *Englewood Cliffs, New Jersey: Prentice-Hall, 1982, p. 117*

In this scenario B.F. Goodrich failed abysmally in its responsibility to develop a quality product for the Air Force. But no individual employee in the organization felt that he or she was violating any such responsibility, and in the end no individual employee felt that he or she was to blame for what happened.

Working for Change

The lack of communication and coordination within the corporate hierarchy at B.F. Goodrich is not uncommon among large corporations, as many readers of this book will attest. And it is not easy to prescribe a set of structural changes that will guarantee that nothing of this sort will happen again.

Nevertheless, Christians and others who are concerned about good ethics in business must not despair. The General Dynamics Corporation, found guilty of improper billings of an almost unbelievable 224 million dollars, took a number of decisive steps to promote a greater sense of ethical awareness and accountability among its employees. First of all, this firm has appointed a full-time Corporate Ethics Program Director (who reports directly to the Chairman) and full-time Ethics Program Directors at each of its divisions. A written code of ethics, with clear assignments of the responsibility of staff members, is distributed to all employees. Also, all employees attend training programs in ethics and are reminded periodically through communications from the program directors of their obligations under the company's code of conduct.

Establishing a good moral climate in a business organization, large or small, takes purposeful, decisive action by those in authority. Christians in business can and have played strategic roles in taking such action both in large corporations—such as Borg-Warner, Donnelly Mirror, and Herman Miller—and countless small companies. The Christians who have exercised this type of leadership frequently share their ideas and insights with others in the Christian business community through books, articles, and lectures. (For those wishing to learn from these ideas and insights, a particularly good place to begin is Max De Pree's book, *Leadership Is An Art*, cited below).

SUGGESTIONS FOR GROUP SESSION

Opening

Read Philippians 4:8–9. In their dealings with shareholders, unions, competitors, and governmental agencies, Christians in business will do well to consider the virtues listed in verse 8 and, as verse 9 instructs, put them into practice.

For Discussion

1. A citizen of Eastern Europe once said: "Under capitalism, man exploits man. Under communism it is the other way around." Evaluate that statement.

   Why should or shouldn't Christians in our culture be striving to establish a communal-style economy, such as the one described in Acts 4? Discuss what it would be like for a group of Christians in contemporary North American society to share all things in common.
2. Discuss honestly your perceptions of organized labor and the unionized worker. Try to identify any unfair biases or prejudices you may have about the unions, and as a group discuss both the good and bad points of these powerful organizations.
3. Some Christians in North America are members of Christian labor unions. Do you think that this is a desirable option? Defend your answer.
4. You are the owner of a sporting goods store that has been prospering in recent years. The only other sporting goods store in town is doing so poorly that it's on the verge of closing its doors. With it out of the way, your store would be even more prosperous. You are quite certain that a spectacular sale supported by a

lavish advertising campaign would finish off your competitor once and for all. Though costly, it would mean increased sales for the indefinite future. Do you go ahead with this plan?

5. When Japanese General Yamashita was on trial for war crimes after World War II, he defended himself by pointing out that what his soldiers did in the Pacific islands was far removed from his command headquarters. According to his testimony, their misdeeds occurred despite his own good intentions. If you were sitting on the war-crimes tribunal, why would or wouldn't you find the General's argument convincing? How might the top management at B.F. Goodrich have constructed a similar defense following its engineering department's falsification of test reports for its new brake assemblies?
6. Discuss the responsibilities of firms toward their suppliers in the light of the following statement by LaRue T. Hosmer in an interview he conducted:

> This company has started to play hardball with our suppliers. People in purchasing think nothing of calling up a supplier we've worked with for years, and telling the supplier it has lost the business unless we get a 7 per cent price reduction. Generally we can't make the parts at the prices that purchasing demands, so it is an empty threat. But the supplier doesn't know that; they'll come back with a 3 per cent reduction, we'll compromise eventually at 4.2 per cent, but we've started to drive somebody else out of business.
>
> —The Ethics of Management, *Homewood, Illinois: Irwin, 1987, p. 198).*

Do you believe this "hardball" attitude is common in the way business is practiced in North America? Give some examples to support your answer. May a Christian participate in practices of this nature?

Closing

Pray that in all things we may learn to love our neighbors—including those we compete with and those who sit on the other side of the bargaining table—as ourselves. You may also wish to sing a closing hymn together. The following would be appropriate and meaningful in the context of today's discussion: "What Does the Lord Require" "The City Is Alive, O God," "As Stewards of a Vineyard."

RESOURCES FOR FURTHER STUDY

De Pree, Max. *Leadership Is An Art.* East Lansing, Michigan: Michigan State University Press, 1987.

Fles, Herman. "Calvinism and Contemporary Business Endeavor," in *God-Centered Living.* Grand Rapids, Michigan: Baker, 1951, 201.

Mellema, Gregory. "Sharing the Blame," *The Reformed Journal,* XXXIII (1983), 11–13.

Williams, Oliver and Houck, John, editors. *The Judeo-Christian Vision and the Modern Corporation.* Notre Dame, IN: Notre Dame University Press, 1982.

SESSION SIX

WORKING FOR A BETTER FUTURE

The previous chapter concluded by describing the General Dynamics Corporation's attempts to bring about a greater awareness of good values and a heightened sense of moral accountability among its employees. Fortunately, General Dynamics is not alone. In a day and age in which the modern business organization is viewed with great cynicism and distrust by the public, many business executives have begun to realize the need for better values and higher ethical standards. As a result, in recent years many business organizations have formally adopted codes of ethics, sponsored seminars on ethical issues for their employees, or hired full-time officers to promote corporate ethical awareness. Often it has been Christians in these organizations who have been instrumental in bringing about these changes.

More firms than ever before have turned their energies in the direction of corporate social responsibility. A study by Eilbert and Parnet reveals that over 90 percent of the largest corporations in the United States have now assigned formal responsibility for such issues to either an officer or a high-level committee. Prior to 1965 less than 20 percent of these firms had such a position. The Weyerhaueser Corporation goes so far as to commission a well-respected person outside the firm to prepare a formal criticism of Weyerhaueser's social policies, and actually publishes this criticism in the company's annual report.

Developing a Code of Ethics

The codes of ethics that business organizations adopt vary widely in content and specificity. Some are so vague that they can hardly be of any real use. Others, as one critic puts it, function only as "so much moral eyewash." But some corporations have gone to great trouble to write codes that will genuinely make a difference in the moral atmosphere of the workplace.

In 1982 the Borg-Warner corporation adopted "To Reach Beyond the Minimal," an excellent example of what a corporate code of ethics can be. Its basic premise is that while there is a minimal standard of what is ethically permissible, those employed by Borg-Warner are encouraged to rise above this standard in the pursuit of moral excellence. Following are some excerpts from this code.

> Any business is a member of a social system, entitled to the rights and bound by the responsibilities of that membership. Its freedom to pursue economic goals is constrained by law and channeled by the forces of a free market. But these demands are minimal, requiring only that a business provide wanted goods and services, compete fairly, and cause no obvious harm.
>
> For some companies that is enough. It is not enough for Borg-Warner. We impose upon ourselves an obligation to reach beyond the minimal. We do so convinced that by making a larger contribution to the society that sustains us, we best assure not only its future vitality, but our own . . . .
>
> We believe in the dignity of the individual. However large and complex a business may be, its work is still done by people dealing with people. Each person involved is a unique human being, with pride, needs, values and innate personal worth. For Borg-Warner to succeed we must operate in a climate of openness and trust, in which each of us freely grants others the same respect, cooperation, and decency we seek for ourselves. We believe in our responsibility for the common good . . . . Our challenge is to supply goods and services that are of superior value to those who use them; to create jobs that provide meaning for those who do them; to honor and enhance human life, and to offer our talents and our wealth to help improve the world we share.
>
> We believe in the endless quest for excellence. Though we may be better today than we were yesterday, we are not as good as we must become . . . . None of us can settle for doing less than our best, and we can never stop trying to surpass what already has been achieved.

Recognizing Christian Values

Whenever a firm undertakes to provide clear moral guidance for its employees, it does so by calling attention to a number of values that it believes are of critical importance. For Christians, these must be values that are rooted in Scripture.

In their book *Full Value*, Oliver Williams and John Houck highlight seven biblically based values that they believe are formative of the Christian way of life and therefore ought to be operative in the lives of Christians in business. For each of these seven values they present a "contrasting" value associated with a secular or humanist perspective that Christians in business ought to resist.

Power Over Others

The Bible teaches the value of using power over others to help them develop their unique gifts (Phil. 2:1–18, John 13:1–17). It is not wrong, in and of itself, to have power over others; it is only wrong to misuse such power. Christians who have power over others must recognize and value this power as an opportunity to help others develop their own gifts.

In contrast, the secular mind often views power as a means of dominating and controlling others. Christians entering a business career discover very rapidly that this attitude is almost taken for granted in the way many people in North America operate in business. Such Christians may be very tempted to pretend there is no conflict between the Christian and non-Christian views of power—but in so doing, they ignore a value set forth in Scripture.

Power Over Nature

The Bible proclaims the value of using power over nature as a means to exercise stewardship over God's world. Humans have been given the responsibility to transform nature in harmony with the whole of creation (Gen. 1:26–31). In business, as in all other walks of life, people have an opportunity to enjoy and make use of the good gifts God gives them through nature, but these gifts must be used responsibly.

In contrast, many people understand power over nature as a mandate to produce a maximum of consumer goods and creature comforts. It is this conception of power over nature that permeates North American culture, and it is easy to internalize this value in our lives and business practices.

Using Wealth to Serve

Christians should view wealth and property as opportunities for increased service for humankind. Scriptures teach that although wealth and property can constitute a possible obstacle to salvation, they can also provide a good way of increasing our service to others (Luke 12:13–21, Luke 16:19–31, Mark 12:41–44). Through the use of its wealth, for example, the business organization not only provides people with the means to earn a living but also helps them fulfill the basic human need to make a meaningful contribution to society.

To the secular mind, in contrast, wealth and property are valued as the sole measure of a person's worth. Clearly, this notion of wealth and property goes against everything that Christianity stands for, and Christians in the business community ought to challenge this value whenever and however it manifests itself.

Finding Happiness Through Obedience

Christians learn that one finds happiness through following God's intentions for humankind (Mark 8:36). The person who lives in accord with God's will for his or her life will unquestionably experience a deep sense of satisfaction and fulfillment. To many who look back upon a long, successful career in business it is acting in accord with God's will which has provided the greatest satisfaction, even though doing so meant making some short-term sacrifices.

The world's contrasting value is the achievement of happiness through acquiring possessions. North American culture places a strong emphasis upon equating happiness with material gain.

Seeking Justice

Christians must work for justice. Scripture depicts justice as the fundamental right of each person to life and the means of sustaining life (Acts 2:42–47, Lev. 25, Gal.3:27–28). To deprive others of justice is a violation of Garrett's second test, for such actions strike at the very dignity of the person. We must keep this biblical model of justice before us as we work to promote justice and fairness in the marketplace.

From the secular perspective, justice is merely the protection of property already possessed. According to this view a system of justice is necessary first and foremost to prevent others from seizing the property one has accumulated.

Denying Self

The Bible teaches that we should be willing to defer the gratification of our own wants for the greater good of society (John 12:23–26, Luke 14:27, Matt. 10:39, Matt. 16:24). Those who practice true discipleship will find it necessary to deny themselves, take up their cross, and follow Christ.

The contrasting value here is the immediate gratification of wants. More than in any other period in history, a desire for the immediate gratification of wants appears to have embedded itself into the mindset of contemporary North Americans. It is evident not only in the lifestyles of individuals, but also in the way many entrepreneurs, managers, financiers, arbitrators, takeover artists, and shareholders go after quick and easy short-term profits rather than pursue alternatives which—though they bring greater long-run benefits to society as a whole—also involve deferring personal gratification.

The Importance of Time

Christians need to recognize the value of time. The Bible portrays the value of time in terms of reverence to God (Luke 12:22–32). Those who take time to be holy are honoring time in the way God intends.

To the secular mind, time is money, and thus pursuing the values discussed earlier is a waste of time. But some of the most successful Christians in the business world have resisted living by the dictum that time is money and, recognizing the wisdom of Christ's words in Luke 12, have found the time to be of service to others, to exercise stewardship, and to pursue justice.

A Less Greedy Future?

Williams and Houck concede that Christians who make an honest effort to live in accord with biblically based values such as these might very well fail to be considered successful in their business careers. Measured by worldly standards of success, such Christians might fall short. They cite a study which suggests that frequently the corporate system screens out people who have much to contribute but who, since they are generous and compassionate, tend to be considered weak or unfit.

On the other hand, there seems to be a growing realization among many leaders in the business community that good values can work to improve the integrity of the organization. They are beginning to see that it is ultimately counterproductive to hire only those whose vision is narrowed to fit the firm's limited objectives. It doesn't take a great deal of insight to see that it is neither good ethics nor good business to demand this narrowness of vision of those who are hired or promoted to positions of responsibility.

There also seems to be a growing realization among leaders of the business community that it is ultimately counterproductive to permit greed to be the driving force in business. In August 1989, *Fortune* published an article entitled, "Is Greed Dead?" The article cites a survey which suggests that three out of four working Americans between the ages of 25 and 49 would like to see the country return to a simpler lifestyle with less emphasis on material success. The suggestion is that younger working people are becoming increasingly disenchanted with greed and with the idea that a person's worth is measured by the wealth he or she has accumulated.

In another survey, working Americans were asked to identify the most important indicator of success. Only 10 percent of those surveyed responded that earning a lot of money was the most important indicator, while 62 percent responded that a happy family life was the most important indicator. The article also cites evidence that men and women are becoming more and more interested in performing volunteer work. People have a growing sense that there is much more to life than the accumulation of wealth, and many are finding, as Christians have known all along, the truth in a statement made by President Bush soon after his inauguration: "From now on, any definition of a successful life must include serving others."

A century ago nearly every powerful person in business believed that the marketplace had no room for values of the sort discussed by Williams and Houck. Typical of the nineteenth century was this statement by Dan Drew, founder of Drew Theological Seminary:

> Sentiment is all right up in the part of the city where your home is. But downtown, no. Down there the dog that snaps the quickest gets the bone. Friendship is very nice for a Sunday afternoon when you're sitting around the dinner table with your relations, talking about the sermon that morning. But nine o'clock Monday morning, notions should be brushed aside like cobwebs from a machine. I never took any stock in a man who mixed up business with anything else. He can go into other things outside of business hours but when he's in the office, he ought not to have a relation in the world—and least of all a poor relation.
>
> —*Quoted in Robert Bartels, ed.,* Ethics in Business, *Columbus, Ohio: Ohio State University Press, 1963, p. 35*

The Wisdom of the Golden Rule

Obviously, the view that good moral values should not be excluded from business life is still very much in evidence in our society. However, it is much less common today than it was a hundred years ago, and there are signs that it may be in a period of further decline in North America.

This booklet began with the story of a grain merchant deciding whether to inform the starving townspeople that more grain was on the way. One retired Christian executive, upon being presented with this story, remarked that he discovered early in his career that the Golden Rule is frequently the best way to approach moral dilemmas such as this. Applied to this case, the Golden Rule seems to indicate that the merchant *ought* to inform the townspeople—just as he would wish to be informed if he were one of them.

Perhaps many of us have a tendency to underestimate the degree to which the Golden Rule can be of help to Christians in solving moral dilemmas. According to Christ's words in the Sermon on the Mount, this rule sums up the entire law and the prophets. The Golden Rule is also one of the most enduring of all ethical standards, not only in Christianity but in most of the world's religions. Says Craig Lundberg in an article in the *Economic and Business Bulletin* (January, 1968, p. 36):

> In the Talmud, for example, we find, "What is hateful to you, do not to your fellow man." Confucianism, too, in the Analects has, "Surely it is the maxim of loving kindness: do not unto others that you would not have them do unto you." Buddhism in the Udana-Yarga says, "Hurt not others in ways that you yourself would find hurtful." Islam joins the chorus with, "Not one of you is a believer until he desires for his brother that which he desires for himself." And in the Mahabharata the Brahman injunction says, "This is the sum of duty: do not unto others which would cause you pain if done to you." And so we see that the Golden Rule exists throughout the major religions of mankind.

Christians who seek to do the good and right thing in business are painfully aware that there is no simple formula that will always yield the perfect solution. Sometimes Scripture itself offers a clear solution, and sometimes one's conscience yields clear direction. In many cases, one may find valuable guidance from the pursuit of biblically-based values, such as those to which Williams and Houck call our attention. At other times one might find valuable guidance in applying Garrett's five tests. But when all else fails, one will frequently find the solution in the wisdom of the Golden Rule—a truth that many people in various religions have known for centuries.

By applying this rule and allowing their faith to bring focus to all their dealings and decisions, Christians in business will begin to make a difference in the marketplace. Perhaps the issues introduced in this booklet will lead to a greater awareness of the ethical problems in the way North American business is routinely conducted. And perhaps they will stimulate Christians to take an active hand, as transformers of culture, to go out into the world in the name of Christ and claim all areas of life, including the area of business, in his name.

SUGGESTIONS FOR GROUP SESSION

Opening

Begin this session by reading Matthew 7:11–12. In his Sermon on the Mount Jesus directs us to give good gifts to others and to do to them what we would want them to do to us. This rule, he says, sums up the law and the prophets.

Think of situations you have encountered during the week in which you might have applied the Golden Rule. Share these experiences with the group.

For Discussion

Throughout this booklet, emphasis has been placed upon the responsibilities of business organizations and those who are employed by them. However, as consumers of the goods and services produced by business organizations, all of us have responsibilities to practice good ethics. The questions in this lesson are designed to address this dimension of business ethics.

Discuss each of the following mini-cases and explain why a Christian could or could not approve of what is done.

1. After waiting in the checkout line for fifteen minutes to pay for his purchases, Dirk finally gets his turn. The total on the cash register seems on the low side, and after paying for his purchases, Dirk discovers that he has indeed been undercharged by a dollar. Straightening out the mix-up would require going to the back of the line, which is now at least as long as it was before.

   Dirk decides that he is not willing to go to the trouble of getting in line again to straighten out a one-dollar mistake. He is angry for having to wait so long in line, and he can barely stand the thought of doing so again. Besides, on one previous occasion when he pointed out a similar mistake, he had angered and humiliated the clerk.
2. A few weeks later, Dirk is again undercharged by a dollar, this time in a restaurant in another city. He is in a great hurry and is unable to take the time to straighten out the mix-up. So he simply leaves an extra dollar next to the already generous tip he has left for the waiter.
3. Henrietta phones an order into a take-out restaurant. She informs them that she has a coupon that will entitle her to a discount. When she picks up her order, she is charged at the discounted price but no one asks for her coupon. Henrietta

decides not to say anything about the coupon so that she can use it again on a future occasion. She rationalizes her actions by telling herself that the restaurant probably doesn't care. If they did, they would certainly have asked her to produce the coupon.

4. In a crowded restaurant, Bill notices that some people from another table are helping themselves to beverage refills to which he knows they are not entitled. Bill considers reporting them to management, but he decides not to, reasoning that it is none of his business.
5. At a high school football game Kay sees that her son and several other boys are accepting great quantities of free food and drinks from a friend of dubious reputation who has temporarily been placed in charge of the refreshment stand. Kay thinks about interfering, but she doesn't want to create a scene.
6. A land development company invites people to a weekend retreat in the hopes that its guests will purchase parcels of land or vacation homes. George has no interest in making any such purchase; in fact, he lacks the financial resources to do so. But he and his wife nevertheless enjoy the weekend retreat and try to act interested during the sales presentation. They feel a bit guilty, but they reason that the company is well aware that many of the guests are not interested in buying anything. They figure that to the salesmen, they are no different than the other couples at the retreat. What the company doesn't know won't hurt them.
7. When Todd moves into his apartment, he discovers that an entire closet is occupied by unopened cartons of brand-new televisions, VCRs, and stereo components. When he complains, the landlady tells him that the previous tenant had to leave town in a hurry and said she could have them. She encourages Todd to sell these items to his friends for whatever he can get and split the proceeds with her. Todd is suspicious, and he wonders whether the equipment is "hot." But he is short of cash and he follows his landlady's advice, rationalizing his actions on the basis that he cannot prove that they were stolen. Within a few days all the merchandise is sold, and Todd's share of the proceeds is nearly $700.

Closing

As a group, evaluate the six sessions you have had together. Was the content meaningful and relevant? Did it help you to rethink some of your behaviors and resolve to make some changes? What else might have been included in your discussion about business ethics?

If the group has quite a few ideas for further discussion, you may want to continue meeting for a few more weeks. If so, you may want to consider using videos (available through Travarca) to help structure additional sessions. *Called to the Marketplace* (InterVarsity, four parts, each 25 min.) explores the dynamics of living the Christian faith in the workplace. *Ethics in America* (PBS specials, 11 titles, one-hour each) features nearly one hundred panelists who tackle highly-charged current issues in various fields of ethics: personal, business, medical, media, judicial, and military.

Close with prayer, asking God's blessing on business leaders who are making an honest effort to promote good values in their organizations. Pray that their example may have a positive impact upon their employees and may serve as a good example to others in positions of leadership.

RESOURCES FOR FURTHER STUDY

Beisner, E. Calvin. *Prosperity and Poverty*. Westchester, IL: Crossway Books, 1988.

Houck, John W. and Williams, Oliver. *Full Value: Cases in Christian Business Ethics*. San Francisco: Harper & Row, 1978.

Maltby, Daniel. "The One-Minute Ethicist," *Christianity Today,* February 19, 1988, p. 26.

Van der Walt, B.J., ed. *Window on Business Ethics: A Challenge to Christians.* Potchefstroom, South Africa: Institute for Reformational Studies, 1993.